HOW TO GIVE A HOME-RUN HOMILY

HOW TO GIVE A H⚾ME RUN Homily

A Hard-Hitting Guide for Preachers, Teachers, and Soul-Reachers

S. JAMES MEYER

TWENTY-THIRD
PUBLICATIONS
twentythirdpublications.com

TWENTY-THIRD PUBLICATIONS
One Montauk Avenue, Suite 200
New London, CT 06320
(860) 437-3012 or (800) 321-0411
www.twentythirdpublications.com

Cover image: ©Shutterstock.com / photastic

ISBN: 978-1-62785-613-3
Printed in the U.S.A.

 A division of Bayard, Inc.

CONTENTS

Upfront

"WELL, YOU WENT YARD WITH THAT ONE, PADRE," the tall man in the Michigan State pullover whose name I didn't know towered over Fr. John by nearly a foot.

"OK...I don't know what that means, but let's pretend it's good," Fr. John responded with a polite but confused smile.

"I'm talking about your homily, Father. You parked it in the cheap seats," the man extended the metaphor in a way that managed to further obscure the point. Still, I was with him one hundred percent.

Leaning in, I nudged the conversation forward, "Indeed. Your homily was a home run. You knocked it out of the park. Thank you."

The Spartans fan moved on, leaving me with the deeply compassionate and insightful man who would become my spiritual director, mentor, and treasured friend. "Thank you," he said as he took my out-stretched hand in both of his. Then with a bit of a chuckle he added, "Sometimes the Scriptures throw curve balls, so you take your best swing and hope for the best. Maybe I got lucky."

I was struck by the understated confession in those words,

but I also knew it wasn't luck. It was the result of preparation, discipline, focus, and a deep spiritual life. This is true, I suppose, of any real professional. Surgeons, electricians, teachers, accountants, delivery drivers, and chefs don't just show up and take a blind swing, hoping to get lucky.

Fr. John played the analogy forward. "When you say a homily is a home run, what does that mean?"

It was a brilliant question. What defines success at the highest level? I am reminded of the woman who shook my hand after Mass and enthusiastically said, "That was a great homily! I agreed with every word!" At the time, I was taken aback. Is that what makes a homily great—that people agree as though you are expressing an opinion about installing new carpet? I had never thought of a homily as an op-ed. So what makes it effective? Should it be affirming, challenging, inspiring, reflective?

When I think of the greatest homilies I have heard in my lifetime, they all have one thing in common: they didn't just *hit home* with me; they *went home* with me. Literally. Something about them stuck, took root, and deepened the way I understand my relationships with self, neighbor, society, creation, and God. Some were indeed affirming, but most were something else. They were surprising and fresh, as well as being challenging, inspiring, and reflective.

A home-run homily clears the fence around the churchyard. It slips into pockets, purses, and gloveboxes and literally goes home with people. They think about it as they brush their teeth. They dunk their cookies in it and bring it up in conversation during the course of the week. It is memorable, even experiential, and people want to share it with others. And like home runs in baseball, it gets people on their feet. They leave church with new life in their legs, ready to march forward and actively be the hands and feet of Jesus.

I've given a few home-run homilies along the way, many of which surprised me. People will bring them up years later, sending me back into my files to find the homily they're referencing so I can recall whatever it was that worked. It's like watching old game film.

Most of my experience with homilies, however, has been as a pew-dweller, so my expertise is certainly more as a listener than as a preacher. I've done the math and estimate I've listened to approximately 2,750 homilies. Some stuck. Most didn't. But along the way, a few cleared the churchyard fence in a way that was life-affecting, even life-changing. After I was ordained to the permanent diaconate, that became my gold standard: get the shadow of myself out of the way so the inspiring light of wisdom could change lives.

In responding to the call to write this book, I wanted to do so from the perspective of the people who plop in the pews Sunday after Sunday, people with whom I share a sacred kinship. We are the hungry yearning to be fed. In marketing parlance, it's a pull strategy rather than a push strategy. Instead of pushing messages at people, telling them what we want them to hear, we as preachers have a sacred opportunity to respond to the hopes, dreams, anxieties, stresses, and general context of real lives. The result is far more relevant and compelling.

Think of it as carrot cake.

After considering the homilists who have most effectively inspired deeper growth in the lives of people, I'm convinced there is no universal recipe for a great homily, no "Three Easy Steps to Rock Hard Abs" that applies to preaching.

It doesn't work that way. Great homilies are more art than science, and every preacher needs to work on his own individual stroke, like a golf swing or a secret salsa recipe. Please keep that in mind as you read the pages that follow. The invitation is to consider how you might adapt and incorporate these ideas, not how your preaching style should become them. The unique voice and giftedness that God seeks to express through you remains paramount.

My dad used to turn his hearing
aids off during the homily.

"Nothing is better than a bad
homily," he'd say wryly.

Indeed.

If you can't deliver more depth
than silence, choose silence.

Your listeners will
reward you for it.

Start with Energy

PEOPLE LEAVE FOOTBALL GAMES EARLY. It's crazy. Just clear the cobwebs and try to wrap your brain around this: Reasonable people who are allowed to have credit cards, operate heavy machinery, and fix the brakes on your car will plan for weeks, spend $150 or more per ticket, put on special clothes, and arrive at the game three hours early, where they drop another $50 for parking, $20 for a hamburger, and a semester's worth of college tuition for a beer. But it's worth it! They're so excited; this is an event! These are the moments that make memories. Then—hold your breath for this—if the game is disappointing, they go home after the third quarter and mow the lawn. Boom. Just. Like. That.

See, they come with an expectation, specifically an expectation that the game will be engaging and the experience will be rewarding. They've invested a lot of their time, passion, and money. They expect something in return, and when they don't get it, they try to get some of their own life back, even if it's the mow-the-lawn part of life.

Compare that to Sunday morning. This is sacred time

for people and families. After a hectic and often stressful week, a week riddled with dental visits, cold French fries, and a toxic stream of angry news, they want to get some of their life back; they want to reroot and breathe. So they come to church. Or not. Increasingly, they are taking sabbath in a fishing boat, online, or at a local coffee shop with Sunday morning jazz, a blueberry scone, and good conversation. Contrary to conventional thought, the question isn't *if* people celebrate sabbath; it's *how* they choose to celebrate it. They're seeking renewal of spirit, rejuvenation of heart, and inspiration of mind. They're seeking something they can carry with them into the week ahead, a spiritual snack they can pull from their pocket like a box of raisins and chew on from time to time. It might be challenging, it might be comforting, but it's always nourishing. When they do come to church, this is the expectation they bring with them. It's the expectation they place on the homily, and if the experience doesn't deliver, they leave and try to get some of their life back, even if it's the mow-the-lawn part.

Catholic clergy have long blamed declining Mass attendance on secularization and disengagement from organized religion. That's a bit convenient. We blame the masses like lackluster playwrights, so we don't have to admit to a lack of inspiration, relevancy, or energy. Imagine advancing such an argument in any other context.

"Listen, Dr. Amazing Kareenakov, attendance has really dropped off for your lecture and demonstration on the magic of the yo-yo. It just doesn't speak to people anymore."

"That's because they've been lured away by the dark temptations of movie theaters and the bedazzled costumes of Disney on Ice. We need to tell them to come back and rediscover the therapeutic benefits of spinning a plastic disk on the end of a string."

"Well, perhaps they can only watch *rocking-the-baby* so many times."

"It's called *Rock-the-Cradle*. The trick is called *Rock-the-Cradle*. See, this is the problem. You're supposed to be promoting my lecture, but you don't even know the basic terminology."

"That's not the problem. People just don't find it compelling."

"You know, if you actually came to my lecture more than once—and by the way, I saw you texting during the demonstration—but if you had actually listened, you would know that time spent with a yo-yo lowers your blood pressure, but watching princesses with sharp steel blades strapped to their feet fly through the air raises your heart rate. What I do is good for people!"

"Perhaps it lowers their blood pressure because it puts them to sleep."

"So you're saying they just want to be entertained? I'm sorry, but I'm here to educate."

While Catholic and mainline Protestant churches conveniently assign their woes to the notion of secularization (as though engagement with a world beyond church walls is somehow new), interest in spirituality keeps expanding and enrollment at big-box megachurches keeps increasing. What gives? Clearly, the desire for spiritual encounter and growth hasn't waned, nor has the appeal of sabbath. What has changed is that people have become empowered and have gone shopping. Some are finding their sabbath at Starbucks, others on a yoga mat in the park, others at a *Six Flags Over*

Jesus megaplex, and still others with a bagel while watching Oprah's *Super Soul Sunday*.

For those who understand the experiential and spiritual depth of Eucharist, it might be very difficult to imagine how any of these other roads lead to a truly meaningful encounter with sacred mystery. Sadly, however, many former regular churchgoers are now out experimenting with other sabbath options for that very same reason: they're looking for a meaningful encounter that their Catholic experience didn't provide. Over the years, I've sat through far too many meetings and presentations that dismissed the rampant spiritual searching and seeking people are doing with a simple handwave usually followed with a comment such as, "People today just want to be entertained. Without Big Bird, they never would have learned to read."

Wow. Just, wow.

I've watched Oprah's *Super Soul Sunday*. It's not exactly *America's Got Talent*. There are no drum kits or praise bands, no dry ice machines, no sequined angelic dancers. No one is swallowing swords, eating fire, or balancing blind-folded over a tank of sharks. It's simply a conversation that opens people up. That's it. People don't want to be entertained; they want to be opened up, engaged, and inspired.

Hold that thought.

A few years ago, a colleague and I led a series of focus groups on the relationship between religion and spirituality, and the role of the local parish in that relationship. Participants were all members of a local Catholic parish, so there were no nondenominational, Protestant, or non-religious participants. These were all Catholics. In fact, they were mostly happy Catholics, not disillusioned malcontents with axes to grind. Two themes came through loudly, clearly, and consistently: first, spirituality was seen as opening people up while religion was seen as closing people down; second, study participants desperately wanted their Catholic parish to bridge this divide by giving the spiritual piece more weight. A lot more weight. They wanted to be opened up. They wanted a religion that explored more deep, ponderous questions, not one that provided trite, pat answers. This is a very big deal. Even people who were still engaged in their Catholic religion and were coming to Mass every week were saying that they were looking for something more.

Again, people don't want to be entertained; they want to be engaged and inspired.

As a preacher, can you do that? Can you engage and inspire other people? Can you invite them into ponderous, soul-searching questions rather than spoon-feeding trite answers? Gosh, I hope so. That's sort of Homiletics 101, wouldn't you agree? If you are among the very narrow cast of people given the privilege of preaching in a Catholic church or any other Christian church for that matter, you've very likely invested a great deal of your life in studying your material. You know it, you understand it, and everyone sitting in the pews hopes to high heaven you are able to apply it. More on that later. For right now, let's focus on the disposition with which you bring it. Obviously, you have a passion for it. Please tell me you have a passion for it. I mean, you've dedicated your whole life to it after all.

My high school social studies teacher, Mr. Borely, had a passion for basketball. He became a high school teacher so he would have an opportunity to coach basketball, not because he loved teaching. For most of us, it was obvious he found the material to be every bit as dry and uninspiring as we did. He once fell asleep during his own lecture on trade castes in India. Seriously, he started bobbing his head and mumbling his words. Every few minutes he'd suddenly bolt up, shake his head a bit, and blink his eyes rapidly, exactly the way I have in church many times. Finally, he just leaned against the blackboard and stopped talking. We all started laughing. Then the bell rang and jolted his attention. He leapt forward looking confused. After that, we just tried to get him to talk about basketball in every class.

I learned nothing about world cultures that semester, but I learned how to triangulate a defense. Honestly, Mr. Borely was a smart guy. He had the knowledge of the social sciences, just not the passion. Perhaps the most important lesson I gained from him was this: no audience will ever be more engaged by your material than you are. Period. Whether you're an actor delivering a soliloquy, a business-person giving a presentation, a professor offering a lecture, or a preacher sharing a homily, your emotions precede your words. If you're excited, your material will be exciting; if you're reflective, your material will be reflective; and if you're boring, your material will be boring. No one will ever believe in your homily more than you do or be inspired by it more than you are. Period. This is nonnegotiable.

Sit with that thought for a moment. Rest there. Take a deep breath and stare contemplatively at a tree.

You are a conduit of energy and your words are fish or seaweed or discarded cigarette butts that float along in the stream. So be very intentional about your energy. Feed it. Nurture it. Thriving life needs the flow of fresh water. Take your energy for long walks in the woods and share an afternoon with it at the beach. Spend time getting to know it over a glass of wine so that it won't frighten you. Breathe it in; breathe it out. Steep it in your tea. Let the life-giving stream of the Holy Spirit flow through you and water the Christ-seeds preplanted in people's hearts.

Nothing healthy, vibrant, or dynamic is going to flow through stale, skanky, or polluted waters. You know what thrives in lifeless water? Pond scum. No one rubs sleep from their eyes, brushes their teeth, and comes to Mass looking for pond scum. Well, maybe some do. But they are outliers. When I was a kid, we had a woman in our parish who seemed to live for pond scum—Mrs. Sapherady. Everyone, even Fr. Charlie in private conversations, referred to her as Mrs. Severity. Her jet-black hair was wound so tight into a beehive that it pulled her electric blue eye shadow onto her forehead. She was the sort of person who would write to the bishop if Fr. Charlie's knee didn't linger on the floor long enough when he genuflected. After I yawned while serving Mass, Mrs. Sapherady volunteered to be in charge of the Mass servers "because someone has to step up and parent these lazy kids before they all go to hell and take the rest of the parish with them." Then and now, I believe Mrs. Sapherady came to church mostly to have her own spiteful darkness validated. She welcomed pond scum so she could skim it off, hold it up to your face, and growl, "SEE?!" Perhaps if she could just fix all the people around her, she could find peace.

People like that can suck the life out of a preacher. Seriously. If you get two or three Mrs. Sapheradys in a mid-sized parish and they band together, it's exhausting. If these people had been in the crowd when Jesus multiplied the loaves and fishes, they would have grumbled that the bread wasn't toasted, Jesus didn't hold his hands properly when offering the blessing, and the Greenbergs shouldn't have gotten any because they let their son and his illicit wife— they got married on a beach for God's sake!—spend the night together in their home while the younger children were there. What kind of a Christian example it that?! Without even realizing it, you start building a preventive defense into every homily.

Forgive me for sounding uncharitable, and I know I'm being just a little hyperbolic, but this is a big deal. The Mrs. Sapherady mindset represents a very narrow band of Catholic people—two, maybe three percent—but they manage to give themselves an amplified and disproportional voice. It depletes, sullies, and stymies the flow of a preacher's energy, unless...pause to prepare for a reality check...unless the preacher is of the Mrs. Sapherady ilk. Then you basically end up with a dwindling but engaged, self-righteous, often judgmental congregation that prays for all the lost souls they've driven toward other sabbath options.

As an aside, how sincere is a prayer that focuses on what's wrong with other people?

Most preachers are reluctant to break themselves open and pour themselves into a heartfelt homily only to deal with an aftermath of confrontation and criticism. Once after delivering what I thought was a relatively safe but insight- ful homily reflecting on the way the Holy Family shows us that a healthy experience of family is defined by love shared, I was confronted by a man who demanded I be fired (I'm an unpaid volunteer deacon). The accusation: I "reduced" family to love, thereby diminishing the importance of struc- ture, and thus giving permission for homosexual people to enter into family units as long as they love each other. Yup. I didn't make it home in time for lunch that day.

If you've been preaching or speaking in public for more than six months, you've likely encountered Mrs. Sapherady. I'll give you a little space here to disentangle yourself from the memories and shake it off. If you have never been confronted by her, it's likely because: (A) your homilies are so dull even the critics aren't listening (sorry), or (B) you *are* Mrs. Sapherady (even more sorry).

Back on point here: start with your energy, your spirit. Before your assembled or online community receives your words, they receive the energy that flows through you. That's the music on which your lyrics ride. So think of your energy like the dials on a radio: there's a tuner and a volume. The best, most compelling, and engaging preachers are in control of both. For readers who don't remember radio dials, think of your energy as your Spotify account.

Remember, we're talking about energy here, not content. So the idea of a "tuner" refers to the type of energy: reflective, inspiring, joyful, comforting, contemplative, etc. Be intentional about this. When you consider the Scriptures within the context of the day, what is the energy seeking to flow through you into the community?

During the height of the Covid-19 pandemic, a couple of people asked me to preach on the importance of wearing a facemask in public. Fair enough. It was very topical, arguably a respect-for-life issue, and unnecessarily controversial. I prayed about it. At that particular moment in time, however, I sensed the Spirit seeking to bring unifying joy to our community. Because my homily preparation always begins with spiritual discernment, not with content determination,

I knew I had to dial my tuner to joyful hope. The challenge of social responsibility would have to wait for another day.

Likewise, *volume* here does not refer to the volume of your voice; it refers to the intensity of your energy. Some homilies, such as Easter, call for big energy that fills the entire church and spills into the streets outside. Other homilies, such as the one I just mentioned during the height of pandemic, call for a more regulated energy that carries joyful hope to the hearts of people where it can take up rest.

I suppose I should back up and clarify something here. All this talk about energy may have a few people worried that I've steered this train around the New Age bend. Please. The entwined relationship between Spirit and energy goes all the way back to the creation stories, way back to when any idea of new age was, actually, the original new age. It's the breath of life God blows into the lungs of humanity, the blast from angelic trumpets upon Christ's birth, the Spirit that descends like a dove upon Jesus as he emerges from the Jordan, and the tongues of fire that lap down upon the apostles at Pentecost. It's all these things and more. And when you stand in front of a gathered community to offer a homily, it's that same sacred energy that seeks to flow through you. Start there. Begin by identifying and becoming one with the sacred energy that seeks to flow through you.

A Few Things Worth Hanging On To

- People haven't abandoned sabbath. They're looking for a more meaningful and relevant sabbath experience.

- Spiritually seeking people want to be opened up, engaged, and inspired.

- People first engage your energy before ever receiving your words.

- A homilist is a conduit for Spirit, and words are fish that swim in the stream.

- No one will ever believe in your homily more than you do or be inspired by it more than you are.

- Begin by identifying what sort of energy the Spirit is seeking to have flow through you into the community.

Homily as Gift

WHEN I WAS FOURTEEN, I CONVINCED MY SISTER TO SPLIT THE COST OF A BIRTHDAY GIFT FOR OUR FATHER: a beautiful backgammon set. Oh, it was impressive. The leather case was supple, the felt board was soft, and the backgammon stones were smooth and weighty. Mind you, I had no reason whatsoever to think, even for a moment, that my dad would ever want such a thing. He had never played backgammon in his life. I'm not sure he even knew such a game existed. But I wanted it. I wanted to be one of the cool, sophisticated kids in my high school cafeteria who broke out a casual and spontaneous backgammon game. Yes, I was that kind of nerdy. I thought backgammon defined cool. So I convinced my sister to help me buy it—as a gift for Dad.

In fairness, I really did want to play backgammon with my dad. That part was sincere. One of my favorite childhood memories was playing checkers with him on Sunday afternoons. I couldn't have been more than six years old and he'd let me win, giving me an affirming sense of self-capacity. As I moved through middle school and into high school, the relationship I had with my father grew distant, even antagonistic at times. I longed for the innocent closeness we had when I was much younger, when he had no expectations of me other than to be a child. But while that's all true, it was mere rationalization. I gave him the gift I wanted, not the gift he would want.

Looking back on it from over forty years hence, I realize that even the part about wanting to reconnect with my dad was self-serving to a certain degree. I gave him a gift he could use as a portal to enter my world, not a portal through which I would enter his world. In that way, it was arguably a manipulative gift that required him to meet me where I was at, but I was unwilling to meet him where he was at. A much better gift would have been tickets to a Home & Garden Show where I could have accompanied him on a stroll deep into his passions and interests.

As a homilist, this is a huge distinction. Colossal. Hang on.

The whole idea of incarnation—Christ coming to us, for us, among us, within us—is the ultimate gift of a loving, merciful God who wants to enter our world. Not just part of our world, either. All of it. Even the part that's stuck in traffic behind the big truck from Pete's Porta-Potties. This ridiculously incarnate God wants to share our Pringles, watch Netflix with us, cry at our funerals, and sit with us at middle school band concerts. The more you meditate on it, the more it blows your boat right out of the water. At least it should. The ultimate gift in all creation, on earth and in heaven, expresses God's desire to enter our world and companion with us through the grit, briars, birthday parties, and melancholy sunsets. This is the gift of Jesus, the gift of the Word, and the gift of Eucharist. You might want to consider making it the gift of your homily as well.

The direction energy flows through a homily matters. A lot. What happens when we open ourselves to the directional flow of incarnation (God >> humanity) and we resist the temptation to reverse it (God << humanity)? The difference between bringing God to people and bringing people to God might seem like semantics, but it is, in fact, everything. EVERYTHING. There are plenty of other parts of the Mass where the praise energy flows from people toward God. Allow the homily to give space for the Holy Spirit to reciprocate.

We've all sat through homilies and sermons during which a bombastic preacher pounded a pulpit and spoke down to people as if he were a mouthpiece for God on high calling, nay, warning them to stop being so darn human and start acting more, well, godly. To the folks who are torn between paying their rent and purchasing their arthritis medication, the lonely woman whose husband is struggling with depression, and the confused young parents worried about losing their jobs, man, that's a whole lot of nothing. It sure doesn't get them jived to come back next week.

Like Christ himself, the best homilies step down from an ivory tower and order curly fries in places like McGilligan's Gastropub. They mow down popcorn at the movies, stroll through cattle barns at county fairs, and even smile warmly at people in the hellscape called Walmart. This is what Jesus did, right? He hung out with the folks down at the wharf and on the streets. This is foundational to an understanding of the gospel, no? Jesus at a wedding, on the hillside, at the seashore, at a well, at Mary and Martha's house, on the road, in a boat, and on and on. The point here is that Jesus meets people, then and now, as they are, where they are. He doesn't meet them where he is or where he thinks they ought to be. He slides his feet into dusty sandals and enters their world. Shouldn't a homily that reflects on his teachings do the same?

I once heard a priest give a homily about adultery at a First Communion liturgy. Whoa. Can't make this stuff up. The church was packed to the rafters with six dozen eight-year-olds outfitted in full-on Catholic First Communion regalia. Beaming parents, joyful grandparents, aunts, uncles, and cousins packed the pews. For these kids and their families, this was the day the Lord had made! Booyah! They wanted to rejoice and be glad, take pictures, and then go have cake! Clearly, this homily did not meet people where they were. Instead, it challenged all in attendance to come to whatever place, however sinister, that particular pastor was in that week. Now, was the preacher right? Did he make valid points and support them with sound theology? Absolutely. I couldn't argue with any of his content. But being right quickly becomes irrelevant if everyone is tuning you out or, worse yet, sitting in mouth-gaped bewilderment.

Does that mean a homily should never talk about adultery? I don't know. What I do know is that when the scribes and Pharisees brought the adulterous woman to Jesus, he chose the energy of reflection (let the one without sin cast the first stone) for his public comments rather than the energy of correction. He saved correction (go and sin no more) for a private conversation, and then only after he met the woman as she was, where she was, without condemnation.

I really like using the verb "give" with homilies. It reminds us that the homily is, indeed, a gift given through the conduit of the preacher to the community. Homilies are given. They aren't sold to, imposed upon, or hammered into people.

When shared generously and lovingly, homilies are gifts of reflection, contemplation, inspiration, insight, and hope for all humanity. Thus, when preparing a homily, a preacher may be well-advised to follow three foundational rules of good gift-giving:

1. Make it about the recipient, not the giver.

2. Make life better, not harder.

3. Make it something the recipient can use and share.

Make It about the Recipient, Not the Giver

We're so eager to share ourselves. And why not? We're brilliant, good-looking, gifted people with answers to so many of life's most perplexing questions! We've thought about things. We've read books, taken classes, and prayed piously. We've even learned how to navigate traffic circles and we've figured out what's wrong with all the other drivers. How can we hold all this wisdom back? We need to generously sprinkle our insights on the community like baptismal waters at Easter; then they'll know how brilliant and holy we are and how blessed they are to have us serving, nay leading, their parish. Lucky them!

As homilists, we have to be so very careful here. So very, very careful. When preaching, we are facilitating a relationship between the Holy Spirit and God's people. Again, we are merely the pipeline, the delivery truck. The gift isn't even from us; it's through us.

One of the very best gifts I've ever received from my wife

was a set of tickets to see the comedian Jerry Seinfeld. That was Part One of the gift. Part Two was that she would go with me. I'm a huge Seinfeld fan. She is not. And that's why the gift meant so much. It was about me, what I relate to, and what I enjoy, and she wanted to participate in that with me. Seinfeld's routine that night included a great deal of new material focusing on marriage, family, and raising children. Michelle and I both left the theater with eyes watering and facial muscles sore from laughter. It was so relatable to the journey we had been traveling, giving new, joyful perspective on our experience. It was about us.

If Jerry Seinfeld had bemused self-reflectively upon life in New York or the funny things that happen when you're a mega-celebrity, it might have been humorous, but it would not have been nearly as engaging. It wouldn't have been about us, the receivers of his gift.

The best gifts are about the recipients, meeting them where they're at.

Perhaps the worst gift of all is the gift that is not so much about the recipient but rather about the image the giver would like the recipient to become. A classic example is the sports-minded father who gives a football to his nonathletic son hoping it'll spark his interest. Or, conversely, the grandmother who gives her athletic granddaughter a frilly dress that isn't her style at all. However lovingly intended, it's still a backhanded way of saying, "Here's a celebration of the person I'd like you to be." Ouch. This is the apple tree in Eden for a homilist. It's so tempting. It's beautiful, delicious, and juicy—and it will make you feel God-like.

Of course, the counter-rationale here is that the preacher is not telling the community to be more like he (the preacher) wants them to be, but rather to live more in the image of who God wants them to be. Fair enough. But before you hop in that soap box and race it down the hill into traffic, sit under a tree and ponder these two questions: (1) Do I really know who God wants another person to be or where their journey through life is leading? (2) What makes me believe God wants someone to be different than whom God created them to be? Think about Saint Paul and Saint Francis of Assisi. People experience conversions when they're ready and as they're called. A truly pastoral homilist will give the gift of a compass, but never the cudgel of a push. If you push, all you'll inspire is resistance and resentment.

The gift an inspiring homilist offers is twofold. First, it embraces people as they are and where they are, and it journeys forward with them. Second, it orients people toward the light to help them find direction but does not push or coerce them. In so doing, we respect the recipient of the gift and the journey they travel. We help them reframe life as a sacred mystery to encounter and unfold rather than as a problem to be solved or fixed.

Make Life Better, Not Harder

On my son's twelfth birthday, a beautiful Saturday afternoon in June, I drove into the driveway and called him over to my vehicle. Lifting the tailgate, I said, "I got you something special—happy birthday, Jacob."

Imagine his anticipation, his excitement. A gift so big it needed to be hauled in a truck! A special gift from his dad!

Slowly I opened the truck, pausing to look into his eyes. He moved closer. I smiled and said, "I love you, Bud!" Then I opened the truck wide and the sunlight splashed in, reflecting off the bright red paint of a brand-new Toro lawnmower.

He said nothing, merely exhaling and walking away.

To clarify, this wasn't actually his real birthday present. I was just messing with the boy, which is one of the small perks of fatherhood. But he didn't know that at the time. As far as he was concerned, I gave him a gift that was really for me, not him (in that he, not I, would be mowing the lawn), a gift that was from my world, not his, and a gift that would make his life harder.

One of the legendary stories in my family's lore comes from the time my dad brought home the gift of a new puppy. With a toddler in a small apartment and another child on the way, my mother was not thrilled. The idea of managing, training, feeding, and caring for a puppy felt overwhelming. Sure, a puppy was a great gift for the family on one level, but on another level it made life more difficult and complicated. The best gifts make life easier.

When a book about the spirituality of life's transitions showed up in our mailbox one day, sent to Michelle and me by an anonymous gift-giver who was somehow moved, it was the perfect gift at the perfect time. The authors' insights and perspectives gave us context and made life a little easier to navigate during a difficult time. Like the noise-canceling headphones Michelle gave me to facilitate sanctuary on long flights, the gift of a homily should somehow help people out a bit.

Now, easier does not necessarily mean less challenging. When Michelle gave me a subscription to The Great Courses, I was ecstatic. But while much of the material was challenging, the growth and insights ultimately made life easier and more enriching. And, of course, I got to choose my own content and pace, so it wasn't being imposed on my life. Back up with me for a moment. Growth and insight make life easier; lectures about sin and obligation do not.

I'm just going to pause for a moment while readers slam their palms on the table and object. Go ahead. Do it hard enough that the coffee splashes out of your mug and onto the tabletop. There should be a part of you that wants to say, "Back up the wagons, Cowboy." And rightly so.

Reflecting on thoughts and actions that separate us from God (sin) and calling attention to our Christian responsibilities and obligations are certainly part of any comprehensive exploration of what it means to follow Jesus. I'll ride that rollercoaster with you all day long. Just consider three things: (1) No one wants to hear it, especially in reference to themselves, so their defenses go up immediately. Oh, they're happy to hear you talk about what's wrong with everyone else; it's actually validating, but it's not really helpful. Now, does that mean a homily should never go there, that it should never address things such as racism, greed, the devaluation of human life, and so forth? Of course not, but that brings us to the second point: (2) Approach it with a heart pointed at inspiration and growth, not correction. There is a monstrous difference between a homily that says, "Here's a way to live a more whole, integrated, and loving life" and a homily that says, "Here's what's wrong with you; fix it or go to hell." Finally, (3) ask yourself if a homily at Mass is the best place to convey the message. After one particularly grating homily, I asked the preacher where exactly that was coming from. He mentioned that he wrote it in response to a conversation he had with a parishioner during the week. Basically, he tried to convey the last, most authoritative word in a personal argument through a homily to the entire community. Such a homily is not a gift, nor a conduit of Spirit, and it makes life easier for no one other than the preacher.

No one wants to walk out of church on Sunday morning feeling heavy or additionally burdened. If that happens, they're going to start looking for other options. One focus group participant stopped going to Mass because, "That new priest kept telling us we need to do more and give more. I can't." This particular gentleman was working full time and caring for a wife with cancer. He felt defeated when the homilist kept telling him that more was expected. So he quit and made his life easier by opening up his Sunday mornings.

All of this leads to the question, what sort of homiletic gifts make life easier? This would be a good time to get up, stand by the window, and gaze out ponderously while stroking your chin or smoking a pipe, because we're about to get all egghead literary for a minute. It might help if you blow the dust off your freshman English notebook. If you were the kid who lifted his heavy head off the desktop and challenged Sr. Mary Bruno with the question, "When will we ever use any of this stuff in the real world?" well, you're about to get your answer.

Compelling and memorable homilies make life easier by helping to reframe or reconcile archetypal conflicts. Whoa. Sorry about that. My dad drank Schlitz beer and swung a hammer for a living, so I'm a little embarrassed to use words like *archetypal conflicts*. They feel like brand-new dress shoes in hot weather. Really, I'm talking about the grit in everyone's life that causes stress and anxiety, the stuff that holds us back from living freely and lovingly. Great homilies help people figure that stuff out.

You'll recall the five basic story-arc conflicts are: person vs. self, person vs. person, person vs. society, person vs. nature, and person vs. God. Take a deep breath and put down your highlighter. We'll unpack and expand all of that in the next chapter. For now, it's enough to understand that pretty much all of Scripture and, hopefully, all of your homilies help people reframe or reconcile one of these five conflicts.

Make It Something the Recipient Can Use and Share

About a year after I had been ordained, a guy pulled me off to the side after Mass one Sunday morning. He and his wife had three teenaged children and always sat five rows back on the far-left side during our 10:30 Mass. Honestly, rather sadly, that's really all I knew about them. I'd greet them and ask how they were doing, you know, all the topline hospitality stuff. If one of the kids was missing on any given weekend, I'd ask about it, knowing it likely involved a job or a sleepover at a friend's house. But other than coming to Mass, they had no other involvement at the parish, didn't stick around for coffee and cookies, and none of our social circles intersected outside of church, so while I knew of them, I really didn't know much about them. They seemed like a nice but very quiet family.

"Listen," he said as he shook my hand and drew in a little closer, "my kids have always hated coming to church. It's been a fight since they were little. About five years ago, they finally stopped arguing and just came begrudgingly, accepting their fate, I guess."

I nodded. "I'm not sure resigned misery is what we're hoping to achieve here..."

"No-no," he interrupted. "We used to leave here after Mass, get in the car, and drive home in silence. No one said a word. They didn't want to be here, and they sure didn't want to take any of it home with them. But over the past several months, whenever you're preaching, they all get in the car and immediately start talking about the homily. We have a conversation all the way home and it continues through brunch. I'm learning so much about my kids. I just wanted to thank you for that."

Wow. I had no idea how effectively the Holy Spirit was using the conduit of homilies to touch the lives of people even after they leave church. How important is it that a well-crafted homily is carried out the doors and into the world as part of the body of Christ? How valuable is it that a reflection on the word of God continues to nourish people, families, and communities all week long? That's kind of the whole point, isn't it? After all, what good is church that stays in the church?

The best homilies have a *loaves and fishes* quality about them. They are gifts that feed the hungry with substance they can chew on and apply in their own lives, but then they multiply when released into the world. They are gifts people can use to understand their own lives, relationships, and spirituality a little more deeply, and they serve as kindling for meaningful conversations between people out in the world.

A Few Things Worth Hanging On To

- An effective homily, like incarnation and Eucharist, is a gift that enters the lives of people and journeys with them.

- The direction of energy matters—focus more on bringing God to people and less on bringing people to God. They'll find their way.

- A homily should be given to, not imposed upon, people.

- Content should be anchored in and relevant to the receiver's life experience.

- Give a gift that makes life better, not harder.

- Let the homily be a gift that people can actually use in their daily lives and share with others.

Providing Walking Sticks and Sandals

THERE ARE WONDERFUL MOMENTS IN EVERYONE'S LIFE WHEN OUR SOUP IS ALWAYS HOT AND OUR BEER IS ALWAYS COLD. These are the times of great harmony, when the warm sun shines all day and a soothing rain falls overnight, when we ease our feet into cool beach sands and gaze toward an ambiguous horizon across the sea, when we look into another person's eyes and see God's infinite love looking back at us. In these moments, the air is fresh, the wind is calm, and the hot water heater never runs low. Bliss. We love these moments, cherishing them dearly, and we want to capture and hold them forever, posting them on Instagram to let all the world know that life is just as the Creator observed—good, very good.

True contemplatives and mystics are able to live in a constant stream of such harmony with the divine, but they are a rare and treasured lot. The rest of us, pretty much all of us, pilgrim forward in life, catching momentary and fleeting glimpses of this conflict-free wholeness. Our best hope is to encounter these moments more frequently and remain in them a little longer each time. Most of life, however, happens in the broad space between these points of light, where the neighbor's cat visits our child's sandbox and our sister-in-law spreads rumors that our to-die-for lemon cake is from a box.

When people come to Mass, they have this very human habit of hauling all this messy reality with them. They stuff their pockets with anxieties, cram their purses with past trauma, and load their cars with human fragility and brokenness. And they carry every bit of it into church with them, hoping, maybe, to leave some of it behind and go home a little lighter. They come with hope that perhaps they'll hear something, encounter something, or experience something that will help them make sense of things, something that'll help them see how God is present, Christ is working, and the Holy Spirit is guiding them through the conflicted, confusing chaos between their stars.

The people who came out to hear Jesus speak brought these same conflicts and tensions. Such is our human nature. Like us, their conflicts fell into five basic buckets: (1) conflicts with self, (2) with someone else, (3) with society, (4) with nature, and (5) with God. Like us, they were seeking insights that would reframe and reconcile this tension, wisdom that would help them live in peaceful harmony. Always feeding the hungry, Jesus responded by meeting them where they were and nourishing them with parables, beatitudes, and clarity. Whether preaching, teaching, or sharing coffee with a troubled friend, we are invited to do the same, to guide people back to wholeness by helping them reframe and reconcile the conflicts that keep them separated and divided from self, from others, from society, from creation, and from God.

Conflicts with Self

We are duplicitous people. We do crazy, contradictory things, like putting bacon on salads and driving cars to gyms where we walk on treadmills. And we do it all the time. I myself have been a lifelong dog person, but there's always a cat sitting on my desk while I write. Think I'm not confused by this?! I'm a strong advocate for the environment, yet I drive an F150 pickup that gets about nineteen miles to the gallon, and I convince myself it's OK since my wife drives an electric hybrid that gets eighty miles to the gallon. Do you see what I did there, how I made an excuse in order to perpetuate my own inner duplicity? It's in our human nature, I suppose, to rationalize rather than reconcile these conflicts.

Arguably, many of the conflicts in our families, workplaces, communities, and world are merely projections of the conflicts that first manifest within our own selves. Our faith tells us to love our neighbors as ourselves, but our egos tell us to look out for number one and put ourselves first. We pray for peace but harbor anger, we pray for the poor but prioritize our own wealth, and we teach our children to be honest while lying to ourselves about our own addictions and transgressions.

The people Jesus encountered were no different. The rich man who wanted to follow Jesus but could not let go of all the things that possessed him (Luke 18:22: sell all you have and give it to the poor) provides a great example of someone whose ability to enter into full relationship with Christ was inhibited by his own inner conflict.

Without getting into the theology about whether the inner conflict between head and heart, ego and soul, values and behaviors is, in fact, what is meant by original sin, suffice it to say that the people who pile through church doors are bringing all of it with them. It is inherent in each person's brokenness, filling our lives with all sorts of stresses and inhibiting us from living in harmony and wholeness.

These inner conflicts quickly escalate and metastasize as conflicts with neighbors, society, and even God. How can they not? A person who is divided within the self cannot possibly be whole in any other relationship. A gifted, sensitive, and compassionate homilist will reflect on the spiritual implications of all this, inviting listeners to seek personal transformation before trying to change the world. Big bold word of caution here: no one wants to be told that the problem is them, that they're messed up somehow. They quickly get defensive about that and then they shut down. Homilies that help people reframe or reconcile inner conflicts are most effective when they are invitational, not accusatory. They invite people into self-reflection and self-examination, often asking exploratory questions and allowing listeners to discover the answers and insights on their own.

Consider, for example, a reflection on Luke 9:46 in which the disciples argue about who is the greatest. Jesus, of course, raises up a small child and tells them that whoever is least among you is the greatest. It's a wonderful Scripture to invite people into an honest self-examination of their relationship with ego and self-importance. But there are more and less effective ways to approach the topic.

> Less effective: *People today are so full of themselves with their big houses and fancy cars. Everyone wants to be so important. Jesus reminds us that these things actually make us small, not great.*

> More effective: *We all face moments, especially when we're under stress, when we start comparing ourselves to others. Like the disciples in the gospel, we want to raise ourselves up and be superior. Why do we do that? Where do you suppose that need comes from?*

The first example above comes off as judgmental, suggests the problem is social rather than personal, and incites defensiveness among those who like their houses and cars. Arguably, it ultimately divides people between those whom we deem as self-serving and materialistic and those who have somehow managed to transcend this basic tenant of human nature. The second example is empathetic, very personal, unifying, and inclusive—we all do it. Most important, it opens people up to an honest self-examination of what causes this tendency in themselves.

Conflicts with Others

Years ago, the satirical newspaper *The Onion* ran a headline akin to this: "Family Life Found to Be Greatest Threat to Family Values." Ouch. I appreciate such satire because it exaggerates the truth to the point where we can no longer ignore it. In this case, it was biting. Anyone who has been in the pastoral ministry business for more than fifteen minutes winces at the bared teeth of this hard and dark truth.

I recall sitting in a shadowy corner of a local homeless shelter as the clock passed midnight, having a conversation with a middle-aged woman who was experiencing all the anxieties of her first night of homelessness. At one point, I asked her if she had any family living in the area who she might be able to stay with. "Hmmph, family?" she replied. With a sweeping motion, she gestured to all the people sleeping on cots on the gym floor sprawled out before us. There were between sixty and seventy arranged in tidy rows and columns. "Do you think any of these people would be here if they had families? Ha! Family is the reason most of us are here."

Overall, most of the people sitting in the pews on Sunday morning do not have stories so dramatic that they land in homeless shelters. But they certainly all have stories, stories of being hurt by and separated from the people they love the most, or at least would like to love the most. They often hide unhealed wounds beneath stitched-together emotions, finding ways to cope that waver between functional and dysfunctional. From the outside looking in, they may even appear to "have it all together," often because a lifetime of practicing faith has helped them reach a place of tenuous peace. Still, they long to be whole but can only imagine what *being whole* looks like. Mostly, they just want to love and be loved.

If you listen closely to the stories people tell about feeling hurt, wronged, or cheated, the ripeness almost has a smell. The emotions remain immediate months, years, and sometimes decades later. It eats away at our feeling of belonging, our sense of personal dignity, our ability to live in harmony, our access to inner peace, and, arguably, our ability to enter fully into holy communion.

This is the reality many people bring with them to Mass. They are weighed heavily by unresolved and unreconciled conflicts with other people whom, more than anything, they want to be in loving relationships with. They're careful and diligent, however, not to let others see it lest they be judged. Most will sit in stoic silence behind cleanly pressed shirts and under perfectly coiffed hair. They learned at a young age to hide and disguise their brokenness, especially and ironically in church, and it absolutely tints the lenses through which they encounter the gospel.

It would be easy to stop reading here and think, "Dude, you lost me. Most of the people in my parish are from happy, healthy, well-adjusted households. They do not anguish under the fiery breath of the dragon you describe. They are paragons of peace, joy, and harmony." OK, I'll let you have that one, but even they find themselves caught in personal conflicts from time to time. They still struggle mightily with coworkers, resent fellow parishioners who try to control the funeral dinner committee, have disputes with neighbors, and stew over emotionally riddled arguments with their spouses and children.

Unless we find ways to reframe or reconcile them, the conflicts we have with other people deplete love and joy, thereby diminishing our life experience. They drain love from our hearts and deplete our spirits, inhibiting our ability to be Christ to others and see Christ in others.

Of course, there is good news and that's what we're here to preach. The Christian message of mercy and forgiveness offers so much promise and hope, but it's a minefield needing to be navigated with careful steps. When we're the ones feeling heavy with regret and guilt for the things we've said, done, and omitted, well, the promise of God's forgiveness is a bright rainbow against a brilliant blue Sunday morning sky. It's a welcome and restorative promise of new light, new life, and new love. But when we're the ones who have been wronged, the victims of someone else's abuse, addiction, or neglect, hmmm...the call to mercy and forgiveness is a tough pill to swallow. In one study, we had a focus group participant say she left the church when her priest told her she needs to forgive her husband for pointing a gun at her in front of the children. Another said he left after sitting through a homily in which he was told his own sins could never be forgiven until he forgave and reconciled with others—in his case this meant reconciling with a father who abandoned him in childhood, something he was unable to do.

Let's pull this wagon off this detour and back onto the main road. This isn't a treatise on the complexities of forgiveness. It's a book on homilies that advocates on behalf of listeners. Hopefully, you've been reading between the lines and thinking ahead, so you know where this is going. Bottom line: the conflicts people have with other people are very real and very painful. Often, these conflicts have a profoundly negative effect on the totality of self-identity and life experience. People come to church seeking salve and hope. They are hungry for reminders that they are still good and valued people, that these conflicts do not define or diminish them in God's eyes. They also want something good to come from these conflicts, some growth or deep insight that gives the conflict redeeming value.

The Scriptures give us countless opportunities to help people step forward on a healing path that transforms interpersonal conflict into growth. As one example, let's look at the story of Mary and Martha (Luke 10:38–42). The plot is very simple and relatable. Martha is resentful because she's doing all the work while Mary is chilling with Jesus. Who among us hasn't been on both sides of this equation? Again, there are more and less effective ways of unpacking this with a community:

> Less effective: *Martha is so preoccupied with her own busyness, working hard to extend generous hospitality to Jesus, her guest. We all know how much work company can be. Naturally, she grows resentful of Mary who isn't helping. So she appeals to Jesus, who lovingly corrects her, letting her know that presence is the mark of true hospitality. Like us, Martha is challenged to examine her own priorities and forgive Mary for having different priorities.*

Not bad, actually, but...

> More effective: *This one hits close to home for all of us, doesn't it? We've all been there, stewing in our resentment because we're doing all the work while someone else is hanging out and having a good time. That's just parenthood straight up. But it's also marriage, most workplaces, Thanksgiving dinner, and Christmas for a lot of people. In the story, Martha is "doing" while Mary is "being." Martha sees this as unfair, and most of us would agree. That idea of fairness, which of course we only see from our perspective, puts a lot of stress on relationships and households. Jesus reminds us that most of the conflicts we have with other people, especially people we love the most, occur because they don't conform to our expectations of them. But is this really love?*

Jesus points to Mary as an example of how to love someone—just be present and appreciate them without imposing the burden of expectation.

Both of these examples get to the same place, but by different routes. The first example is about Mary and Martha, people who lived long ago in a faraway place. It's easy for listeners to distance themselves. The second example is about us, here and now. Listeners do not have to superimpose themselves over the gospel; instead, they simply apply the gospel to the life they know. But here's where the two examples really diverge. The first sets context and talks about the need for and benefit of forgiveness, but it does nothing to help listeners get past their real-world resentment. Forgiveness remains conceptual. The second example, however, gives the listener insight into forgiveness so it becomes tangible and accessible—perhaps what's straining my relationship with someone is not their behavior but rather the expectations I've imposed without their consent.

It's worth stepping aside for a moment here and noting that this is what causes most conflicts within parish communities as well, isn't it? People impose expectations on their pastors, pastors impose expectations on their congregants, and parishioners impose expectations on one another. People rarely live up to the expectations we have of ourselves much less the expectations others assign to us. No one wants to leave Mass feeling like a failure in someone else's eyes.

Conflicts with Society

In the timeless truth-telling song "High School Never Ends," the band Bowling for Soup captures the painful, universal experience of not fitting in. Through lyrics that shine a light on the world's preoccupation with glamour, celebrity, and wealth, the song masterfully advances the thesis that we never seem to grow beyond the awkward social order of adolescence.

Here's the irony: the experience expressed by the lyrics, the troubled feeling of not fitting into the social order, is so relatable that the song broke into the Billboard Top Forty and stayed there for eight weeks. Rub your head with both hands and think about that for a moment. If everyone feels like the spotted elephant on Rudolph the Red-Nosed Reindeer's Island of Misfit Toys, who actually does fit? Certainly not Jesus—the social order into which he was born ran him out of Dodge ("Truly, I say to you, no prophet is acceptable in his own country"; Luke 4:24).

The need to belong is so foundationally human that Maslow ranked it just above safety in his hierarchy of needs. It is the first, foremost, and most fundamental need once we've met our basic needs for food and water and our need to not be mauled and eaten by a tiger. And yet... And yet it remains elusive for so many of us in our western culture.

People come to church seeking a place to belong, a place where they can be loved and valued for the spotted elephants they are, as they are, at this particular point on their pilgrimage through life. And we make the promise. Our theology is "spot-on" if you'll pardon the pun. We speak of everyone as being created in God's image and likeness, of "catholic" as being universal, of "church" being *all the people of God,* and of Holy Communion as being the *one Body of Christ*. We advocate tirelessly for the dignity of all people, and we offer reconciliation as a sacrament because we acknowledge that everyone is broken, growing, and loved unconditionally.

The insightful, compassionate homilist is well aware of the need people have to belong and feel loved regardless of their imperfections and idiosyncrasies. That same homilist, however, will also be keenly aware of the challenging disconnect between what we as church teach/believe and what people actually experience. Perhaps it'll help if we look at it in a different way. Remember the theme song from the TV show *Cheers*: "Making your way in the world today / takes everything you got / taking a break from all your worries sure would help a lot / ... Sometimes you wanna go / where everybody knows your name / and they're always glad you came." Now imagine walking into this mythical neighborhood pub called Cheers only to discover that it's super stressful and they don't really want you there because your particular spots are the wrong color or too dark or simply too spotty. Why, any one of us would feel deceived and think they're a bunch of hypocrites who don't practice what their theme song promises.

So, yeah...when we're talking about the relationship between people and society, the Catholic Church has a branding problem that homilists are left to struggle with. By *branding problem*, I'm talking about the disconnect between expectations and experiences. Our theology puts one set of expectations into the world (universal, all God's people, every person has value and dignity), but many times our local parish communities tend to deliver a different experience, an experience that is very tribal, often cliquish, and sends an unspoken but clear message that you have to be like us to belong with us. This disconnect goes all the way back to the early disputes between James and Paul: do you have to be Jewish to become a follower of Jesus? You'd think Peter would have solved that issue in a definitive way, but we keep inventing new versions of the question, and it stokes a real challenge for the preacher standing in a pulpit.

This whole point itches me uncomfortably like a large mosquito bite on my soul and, frankly, I'd rather rub some balm on it and make it go away. But it's a contextual reality and homilists need to be as acutely aware of it as Jesus was. There is a significant and vocal swath of every community that is quite confident the homilist's role is to socially and politically validate them and to do so by telling everyone else to think, act, pray, and vote more like they do. The solution to the *person vs. society* conflict everyone faces from time to time, if not all the time, is not to stand behind an ambo and tell everyone that pink spots are acceptable but green spots are not. This is not what Jesus did. He invited, encouraged, and challenged everyone to embrace the person on the margins, the least among us.

If we agree that the Beatitudes express one of the greatest, if not *the* greatest, homilies of all time, then let us look at the social context and what Jesus said. Everyone wanted him to validate their social and political position—the Priests, the Pharisees, the Zealots, the Sadducees, even the Romans—and Jesus responded with *blessed are the poor in spirit...blessed are they who weep and mourn...blessed are they who hunger and thirst for justice.* He did not validate any of them and, instead, advocated for everyone on the Island of Misfit Toys.

The social politics of church pews can be brutal, creating a thorny vineyard for the preacher. A couple of real-world examples: Lost, confused, and grieving following her brother's suicide, a woman returned to Mass after a long absence. On her way out of church, she was confronted by another woman who told her to dress more appropriately if she plans to attend Mass at this parish. She never went back. Another woman, only twenty-eight years old and with four small children in tow, came to Mass in search of support when her husband was imprisoned on abuse charges. More than anything, she needed to be embraced by God's people. Instead, she was admonished and told to "sit somewhere else with your bratty kids." When the Catholic school my kids attended began laying the groundwork for a scholarship program for Hispanic children in the area, I received a call from a prominent "high contributor" asking me to get on board with an effort to kill the program because, "We don't need those kids at our school. They don't belong there. That's not why we pay the tuition." The conversation didn't end the way he had hoped.

These are examples, not exceptions. This sort of social conflict is happening nearly every week in every Catholic parish. People are showing up for Mass with a desire to be welcomed and included just as they are, warts, spots, and all, while also wanting the preacher to validate their desire to exclude and/or correct people who sport spots of a different shape or hue.

So how does a compassionate homilist pick up where Jesus left off in helping people reframe and reconcile this age-old conflict of man vs. society? How do we simultaneously reassure all people that they are loved unconditionally and encourage them to extend that same unconditional love to all others? This issue comes up thematically throughout the gospels in stories like Zacchaeus the tax collector, healing the lepers, the Samaritan woman at the well, and many others. The spirit of these stories gives keenly focused direction to the preacher. In all cases, Jesus leads with love. He opens himself to others, spots and all, just as they are. He has this uncanny and subtle way of disempowering the conflict with society by simply loving the individual! We can do that too!

Let's look at an example: say you're preaching on the story of Zacchaeus. The central conflict in this story is a social one: Zacchaeus, in spite of his wealth, is a social misfit who is shoved to the margins. He has a conflict with society that, arguably, he brought on himself—but that does not stop Jesus from loving and embracing him. How do we help people process this story in a way that enables them to reframe and reconcile their own conflicts with society?

> Less effective: *Zacchaeus got himself into a pickle. Some would say he made his own bed. But that doesn't stop Jesus from loving him, just as our sins don't stop God from loving us. Two things happen here: First, Jesus is open to him and he is open to Jesus. It starts there. Second, he admits his sinfulness and commits himself to correct his ways.*

> More effective: *We've all been on both sides of this equation, haven't we? We've been Zacchaeus, the person on the margins of the playground, the inner circle at work, even the parish community. We've*

been the black sheep in our own families. And we think, if only these people would get to know me. But we've also been the crowd. We've been the people so comfortably embedded in our own community of friends that we start looking for ways to protect our comfort, often by ignoring or even labeling those on the fringes without getting to know them.

The difference between these examples is not in the merit of the point they're making. Both are worthwhile. The difference is in how effectively they engage the listener.

I'm going to pause here for a moment and emphasize a point that is central to this entire book. In fact, if you carry only one thing forward, let it be this: It does not matter how brilliant your point is if no one listens. Period. You can run down to Wild Larry's Ink Emporium and have that tattooed backwards across your chest so you read it every time you look in the mirror. It does not matter how brilliant your point is if no one listens.

Returning to the examples above, the first is churchy and theoretical while the second is real-world and concrete. Start there. Additionally, the first is about some tax collector who lived two thousand years ago, but the second is about all of us here and now. Which do you think your listeners are more engaged by? Finally, when you get done with the first one, people are thinking, "OK, yeah, I got your point. I wish my sister-in-law got your point. That woman needs to sit down with Jesus and admit her sinfulness!" But when you get done with the second one, your listeners are thinking, "Huh, yeah...taking time to get to know people...I hope he unpacks that a little bit." When you speak with contemporary relevancy, people stick with you and tune in to the rest of your homily. There is no hope to reframe or reconcile conflicts if people only listen to the voices in their own heads. When that happens, you as a homilist are not really helping anyone.

Conflicts with Nature

I had an epiphany on the top of a mountain while gazing at the stars. Who hasn't, right? Admittedly, it's a bit of a cliché. Mountains and stars do that sort of thing to people, or perhaps it would be better to say they do that sort of thing *for* people. At the risk of boring you with how unoriginal my spirituality is at times, please allow me to reset. Clearly, if you've read this far, you already know I don't shy away from boring people. Actually, I've been told I'm quite good at it. For the record, however, another way of looking at *unoriginal* is *universal*. Perhaps what I'm about to share is universal to the human experience.

Wild Man Don and I were backpacking in the Cloud Peak Wilderness in Western Wyoming's Big Horn Mountains. If you've read *Jesus Wears Socks with Sandals*, you're already familiar with my brother-in-law, who I affectionately and respectfully call Wild Man Don. He's a corporate accountant whose greatest risk threshold is eating an ice cream cone without a napkin. This makes him the absolutely perfect backpacking companion. He always makes sure we are prepared for everything, including rattle snakes, grizzly bears, and the night sky.

On this particular night, we were camped at 12,500 feet, about three thousand feet above the tree line and only seven hundred feet below Cloud Peak, the highest point in

Wyoming. As the sun was setting, Don was rushing to get things cleaned up for the night. He seemed both anxious and motivated, like a giddy teenager on prom night. "It's going to be a cold, clear night," he said. "We need to lie on our backs and look up at the stars." After a day of hiking up a steep mountain in thin air, I was dog tired, so I happily would have crawled into the tent and simply gone to sleep until the only star in the sky was the morning sun.

But his enthusiasm was contagious, so I followed suit. As I lay with my back against the mountain and my face toward the heavens, there was nothing in my view but an infinite universe. Being so close to the summit, there was no horizon. Being that far into the back country, there was no light but stars. Being at that altitude, the atmosphere was merely a thin and scant filter. With my back against the top of the world, I felt like I was staring into the face of God. In that moment, I simultaneously felt so individually small and insignificant while also feeling part of something so great and beyond the widest stretches of my imagination. It was the spiritual equivalent of sitting in a spark plug's gap, where the Creator's current jolted my spiritual awareness.

Again, this experience was in no way unique to me. It's not original. In fact, it is quite universal. Walking through the woods, gazing at a sunset across the water, hiking through a canyon, standing on a mountain, digging in the garden, staring at the night sky—we've all come face-to-face with the Creator while immersed in the wonders of creation.

Quick side of fries here and then I'll get back to the steak: you cannot credibly preach that which you don't know. And by *know*, I'm talking about human experience and encounter, not merely intellect or academics. There is a temptation to use religion and even clericalism as an escape from the world, but in doing so the preacher disengages from the experience of his listeners. The guy who gets up each morning, gargles with coffee, argues with his middle school daughter about what she's wearing, and goes to a job that drains his soul does not have the luxury of escaping from the world. You can't preach to the fish from the boat; you have to get into the water. OK, back to our main event.

There is a good reason why Jesus went to the mountains and gardens to pray, why he went to the desert to discern, and why he went to the river to be baptized. Our creation stories and faith tradition remind us that we are one with nature (thou art dust and unto dust thou shalt return). We, the created, are woven into the fabric of creation. We breathe its air and drink its water.

There are times when the people sitting in the pews or streaming at home are confused or overwhelmed by a dramatic and life-altering conflict with nature. Cataclysmic events such as earthquakes, tornados, hurricanes, or wildfires that we experience personally or are moved by virtually force us to take stock of human vulnerability. At such times, many people turn to faith to get through, but others will turn away from faith, questioning how a loving God could even permit such tragedy. Most conflicts with nature, however, are more frequent and benign natural events such as thunderstorms and blizzards. People routinely come to church abuzz with stories of downed trees, damaged roofs, flooded basements, heat waves, and the worst malady of all—internet outages. This is topical, on everyone's mind, and woven into the human condition. It's also the time when neighbors lean into each other, but how often do we talk about any of it in our homilies? How often do we help people develop a spiritual frame of reference for dealing with these ordinary but challenging life experiences on planet earth?

Most recently, the global Covid-19 pandemic was, in actuality, a large-scale conflict with nature. Unfortunately, in the United States at least, we turned it into a conflict with society. Perhaps this is because we know how to frame and confront a conflict with society, albeit arguably in dysfunctional and unhealthy ways, but we have no frame of reference for approaching a conflict with nature. We really needed good, grounded preaching not just during the pandemic, but frankly in the years leading up to it. When was the last time you heard or gave a homily that focused on living harmoniously with God's creation or about experiencing human unity with God through creation?

Our central conflict with nature tends to be more passive than active. It feels more like a disconnect than a conflict most days. We go about our business, buying factory-packaged peas off supermarket shelves, completely disconnected from the soil and the seeds. We breathe stale air filtered and pumped through mechanical systems, with no real connection to the trees producing the oxygen we need to sustain our lives. Even our communion wafers, which are supposed to represent the work of our hands, are factory stamped and packaged. Our offering is not the fruit of our labors; it's often just an automatic withdrawal from a bank account and we do it without thinking or connecting it to Eucharist in any way.

What does all of this have to do with a homily? Everything! If we are sincere about wanting to help people reframe and reconcile the conflicts in their lives that keep them divided from each other and separated from God, we cannot ignore the increasing disconnect from creation. The people sitting in Mass listening to the proclaimed word live within the context of a natural order that constantly throws curve balls at them. Cancer, Alzheimer's, Parkinson's, raging teenage hormones, the aging process, peanut allergies—all of it manifests this human conflict with nature that we seldom break open and discuss. Instead, we touch on conceptual platitudes such as *environmental stewardship, God's will,* and *taking up your cross,* which, although having merit in their own right, are a little like handing a hungry man a picture of a sandwich and saying, "Here, think about this." They're great ideas when you're pondering life on a sunny day, but they actually offer very little to help people find a grab bar to pull themselves up in the midst of the storm.

When we're in conflict with nature, we typically benefit from spending more time immersed in or surrounded by creation. There are numerous studies showing that hospital patients in rooms looking out at trees have faster recoveries and better outcomes. The Scriptures we reflect on offer veritable bucketloads of references to Jesus' unity with creation. If he's not knocking around in the wilderness, he's talking about sowing seeds and reaping harvests. Clearly, this is an important dimension of the spiritual practice he exemplified, the stories he told, and the lessons he taught. What a gift we give when we awaken within others the deep awareness of their need for harmony with this same creation!

Consider the story of Jesus' baptism in the Jordan in Luke's gospel (3:22). A more obvious example might be the story about Jesus calming the storm, but let's not take the easy route. At its core, the baptism narrative offers a story of complete immersion in creation in a way that closes the distance between heaven and earth, between body and spirit, between humanity and God. Jesus fills the spark plug gap between the Creator and creation, and the current of Spirit runs through him. I'm not sure I've encountered a homilist who really knows what to do with this story, so most, myself included, build off a small piece of it. We'll talk about the sacrament of baptism, how Jesus is affirmed as the Son of God, and other warm fuzzies. Our gathered communities, always eager to be polite, will sit and smile, feeling good about being in church but actually wondering why Jesus needed to be baptized in the first place. As you've figured out by now, there are more and less effective ways to talk about reframing and reconciling our conflicts with nature.

> Less effective: *Since the fall of Adam and Eve way back in Eden, there had been this separation between God and humanity. We were relegated to this earth to work the fields, toil under the sweat of our brows, and eventually die to this life so we can rise again in the next life. But in the moment of Jesus' baptism, God sends a dove, opens the heavens, and says, "This is my son! I am no longer distant and apart from you. I, God, am now with you and among you."*

> More effective: *Sometimes we divide the world into two tidy buckets. The spiritual realm is good, the earthly realm is, well, if not bad, certainly not as good. Yet where did Jesus go to connect with God? He went to the mountain or into the garden. And*

where did he go for baptism? Not to the Temple, but to the Jordan River. Only by immersing himself in the waters of the earth could he break into the fresh air of Spirit. Farmers and gardeners understand that only by digging into the earth can we cultivate and nurture new life. Baptism connects us to God, not apart from the world, but through the elements of the world. This is the way to wholeness that Jesus shows us through his own baptism. We, too, need to reconnect with God through the elements of the natural world. We need those quiet walks in the woods.

You can wrap yourself in the first example, I suppose, like a child with a security blanket. It's comforting. It's familiar. It's safe. It's also exactly what every person sitting in every pew has heard a hundred times. It's not fresh and it offers no new growth. It's just sort of heady religion, what we've all come to expect, but most people have been conditioned to tune out. It also limits its frame of reference to God and Jesus, offering little to no perspective on contemporary human experience. As a listener, I hear it, but I have no idea what to do with it.

The second example offers a twist that, rather sadly, comes as a surprise to a lot of Christians: "This world, this creation, is sacred?! My personal experience of communing with God through the created world is valid?!" Remember, as homilists, we are aiming to help people reframe and reconcile the conflicts in their lives, the things that keep them divided and separate from one another and from God. Giving them a frame of reference to unify their lived experience in the created world with their Creator is a very compassionate thing to do!

I don't know about you, but I'm feeling like we've earned a little break here. Forgive me if it sounds boastful, but I'm pretty good at recognizing when it's time to take a breather, sit by the well, and chat up the poor and unsuspecting soul next to me. In fact, I wouldn't be shy about listing "break taking" among special skills on my resume. We've traveled a lot of ground in this chapter. Before we take it home, let's uncinch our packs and grab a handful of gorp. For the unfamiliar, *gorp* is a hiker's term for trail mix, usually a mixture of nuts, raisins, and M&Ms. It's break food on the journey. It's also a great opportunity to eat M&Ms and feel healthy about doing it.

Let's just sit on a rock here and take stock of where we've been. This chapter has been a long and winding journey up the side of a mountain called "human conflicts." This is the baggage people bring with them to church, the yuck-stuff that inhibits us from living lives of harmony and wholeness with God and with one another. It's heavy so people want to put it down and free themselves from it, but it's also sticky so they can't. Sometimes, as we discussed, people have been carrying it around for decades, and it has become attached to them like a parasite feeding off their happiness.

We started small with the internal conflicts people have within themselves. Then we journeyed progressively wider through conflicts with others, conflicts with society, and conflicts with nature or creation itself. Why are we doing this? What relevancy does it have to homilies? Well, this is the stuff that weighs people down and holds them back from loving themselves and others generously. The gift of a good homily helps them wash it bit by bit from beneath their fingernails.

The final conflict we need to break open in this chapter is the big one: conflicts with God. Whooo, boy! Grab yourself another handful of gorp, cinch up your pack, and let's finish climbing this mountain.

Conflicts with God

Imagine sitting in a relationship counselor's office with God:

M *(me)*: I just feel like there is an imbalance of power in this relationship.

C *(counselor)*: How do you feel when you hear that, God?

G *(God)*: A little sad. You know, I want there to be mutuality.

M: Well, there isn't. How can there be? You're the Almighty. What you say goes every time.

C: Is that true, God? Do you call all the shots?

G: I don't see it that way at all. SJ has complete free will. Actually, he does whatever he wants whether I approve of it or not.

M: Oh, but you make sure I pay the price afterward, don't you? I feel like you can be manipulative that way. You say I have free will in this relationship, but if my free will doesn't match your divine will, I'd better look out.

C: That's a big statement. It might help if you can give God an example.

M: Alright. How about the time I wanted to go to the playoff games at Lambeau in January, but my wife wanted me to stay home with her and the kids—and you told me to listen to my wife.

C: So what did you do?

G: He exercised free will and went anyway.

M: There. See? Yes, I exercised free will and went to the games anyway, two weeks in a row. And God here tried to make it miserable for me by driving a cold January rain onto the first game, and then followed that by turning the temperatures to fifteen degrees below zero for the second game. But I had a great time anyway.

C: You're holding God responsible for the weather?

M: Please... we're talking about God Almighty here.

C: How do you respond to that, God?

G: Yeah, here we go. It's climate change, man. These humans bring it on themselves. This guy drives an F150 pickup truck that gets only nineteen miles to the gallon, and then he wonders why the weather is erratic. I love you, Bud, but you have to accept culpability.

M: Fine, maybe. But the weather wasn't the real issue. God here made me pay the price for exercising my own free will by giving me pneumonia and strep throat. That's what I'm talking about. God claims I have free will, but when I do what I want, the Almighty here thunders down consequences.

C: Whoa, seriously? God, you gave him pneumonia and strep throat? At the same time? Can you see where he might think that's vindictive?

G: I didn't give him those illnesses. I'd never do that. He did that to himself.

C: Is that true? Do you think maybe you brought that on yourself?

M: Why on God's earth would I do that to myself?

G: I want to go back to something. It's not just my earth. It's yours too. I wish you'd clean it up a bit.

C: God, we'll get to that later. Right now we're talking about mutuality in your relationship.

G: The two are related. Just sayin'.

C: I hear you. And it's important that we discuss it. Right now, however, I'm waiting for an answer from SJ to the question of whether he might have brought the illnesses on himself. Did you?

M: I don't know how. I'm not God.

c: Well, you sat in a cold January rain for four hours and then six days later you sat in below zero windchills for another four hours. Surely, your mother told you that you could get sick from doing things like that.

m: OK, yeah, maybe...

c: Do you think you might owe God an apology for pointing fingers?

It's a weird relationship we have with God. Can we at least be honest about that? Rather than challenging the narrowness of our own human vision and thinking, we often have a way of contorting God into a box that fits the human way we relate to other people. We bring God down to size so to speak, which often works out for us because God is so willing to meet us where we are and work from there.

When people settle in to listen to a homily, they're often living in various dimensions of this conflict. Who is God? What is God? The twenty-four-hour news cycle bombards us with a continuous stream of images of a suffering world that's burning in pain, violence, and injustice. Where is God in all this? When it strikes close to home, it gets personal. How can a loving God let a young mother get cancer? If God is just, how come my amazing and brilliant niece was killed in a car accident at the age of sixteen? We've all been confronted with these questions, wanting so badly to give confident, compassionate answers but knowing that anything we say is inadequate.

The conflict people bring to church with them is often less about the existence of God and more about the nature of God. Certainly, the people Jesus encountered had the same questions and conflicts. His answer, of course, was love. The nature of God is forgiving, merciful, unconditional love. But he didn't just speak it; he showed it so that people wouldn't just hear it, they'd feel it. And that's really the challenge faced by the contemporary homilist, isn't it? Let me echo Maya Angelou again: People don't remember what you say; they remember how you made them feel.

When it comes to helping people reframe or reconcile their conflicts with God, the content of our words will always be colored and even overshadowed by the spirit of our expression. We as preachers cannot explain God to people. How fantastically crazy and even arrogant is that? Who are we kidding? We don't actually know the mind of God. Whenever I hear a preacher talk about what God wants, I roll my eyes. Who among us really knows what God wants beyond love? The people to whom you preach are not children. They are mature, often very mature, adults who have pilgrimed across a lifetime of experience. They know joy and sorrow, laughter and tears. They also know that none of us really understands God.

Here's the thing: As preachers, we tend to come at our homilies intellectually. We want to be apologists and help people understand things by explaining them or, as my wife would say, by man-splaining them, which she means quite derisively. But we know that God cannot be understood intellectually. Our minds are way too small. God can only be encountered spiritually.

I find it quite helpful to think about this when preparing homilies. It is a waste of energy and breath to try to explain God to people, even, perhaps especially, to the faithful. If they have not been able to arrive at an understanding of

God after a lifetime of trials and tribulations, you certainly cannot feed it to them on a spoon in seven minutes. But the far greater gift you can give them is an encounter with God. Isn't that really what Jesus did? Perhaps this is the most powerful and critical question you can ask yourself during your homily preparation: How does this homily offer people an encounter with God?

For that, let's look at the way Jesus encountered people. First, he met them where they are as they are. We covered this in an earlier chapter, but it's worth revisiting. An effective homilist enters the world of the listeners. He might speak of the kingdom of God, but his point of reference is the factory floor, the middle school band concert, and the Starbucks drive-thru, just as Jesus spoke of vineyards, sowers, and mustard seeds. Second, Jesus sat down and broke bread with people. The significance of this is off the charts. By doing so, he gave them dignity and value equal to his own. Now just inhale that all the way into your lungs for a moment. He was JESUS! The Messiah. The Son of God. The Savior of the World. And when he encountered people, he raised them up and eyeballed them with mutual respect and appreciation. The preacher who finds the pulpit to be a platform of self-importance is going to struggle to relate to people. You cannot give people an encounter with God when you perch yourself on a pedestal or regard yourself as more important, more holy, or (watch out for this one) more moral than the people to whom you are speaking. Finally, when Jesus encountered people, he never criticized, condemned, or complained. This is straight out of Dale Carnegie's *How to Win Friends and Influence People*. Jesus was way ahead of his time, apparently. Sure, he criticized some groups of Pharisees a bit, but that was mostly because they consistently violated all three of these rules for encounter: (1) they did not meet people where they were as they were—instead, they told people how they "ought" to be; (2) they would never dream of sitting down and breaking bread with someone they regarded as lesser, and they openly challenged Jesus for doing so himself; and (3) they criticized, complained, and condemned as a routine expression of their faith.

In preparing and presenting a homily that helps people reframe or reconcile their conflicts with God, you would be well advised to be more like Jesus than like those Pharisees. Give people an encounter with God the way Christ did. Meet them where they are, raise them up, and love them. To illustrate, let's look at the Road to Emmaus story.

> Less effective: *We can identify with these guys on the road, can't we? They're feeling lost and confused. When Christ joins them, they're so overwhelmed by things that they don't even recognize him. But later, when Jesus breaks the bread with them, their eyes are opened. They see that it's true—Jesus is in fact risen! How joyful that must have felt! Jesus offers us this same experience when he breaks bread with us here at Mass.*

> More effective: *We can identify with these guys on the road, can't we? They're feeling lost and confused, as we do often. Jesus had given them reason to believe in hope, in love, in mercy. He showed them a compassionate, healing face of God. And now it's lost. Or is it? What can they believe? What can we*

believe? We get so many mixed messages from so many different directions. What's cool about this story is that Jesus walks with them, sits with them, and eats with them as they struggle to open their eyes to the miracle right in front of them, a miracle that's been with them all along and they should have anticipated. Same with us. He just walks with us, listens to us, and breaks bread with us. This is how he brings God to us and how he invites us to bring God to one another. It's a beautiful encounter. Relationship leads to realization. And isn't this the living hope our world needs—for everyone to stop telling everyone else what to think and believe, and instead for all of us to simply walk with each other, listen to one another, and break bread together?

The first example simply frames and explains the gospel story. It's nice, but we've all heard it before. It tells us what Jesus did but doesn't tell us what to do. It does nothing to show us how to bridge the conflicts in our own lives. The second example gives us all something that we ourselves can experience and something we can share. In this way, it transitions the static word into the living word.

A Few Things Worth Hanging On To

- People live conflicted lives and bring those conflicts to Mass with them. They are looking for a homily that helps them reframe or reconcile those conflicts so they can be whole again.

- Invite listeners to seek personal transformation before trying to change the world.

- Give your listeners actionable insights from the Scriptures that they can readily apply within the context of their own relationships.

- You can't fix the world with a homily, but you can help people refocus the lenses through which they see the world.

- Homilies that resonate seek to help people grow toward unity with God, recognizing that the road toward unity with God travels through unity with self, others, society, and creation.

- Trust that people grow into an understanding of God over a lifetime, so you don't have to explain it in a homily. Instead, let your homily simply be an encounter with God.

The Power of Story

When I was sixteen, I'd skulk around the kitchen before supper, trying to get a head start on the roast beef before it hit the table. I often used this time to bait my mother into an argument of one sort or another, a little intellectual garlic to give the ensuing dinner conversation some kick. I figured the least I could do for her was make sure her life wouldn't get boring.

Just as mom was draining the potatoes one evening, I dropped this gem: "You know, I don't think I believe in God. It's kind of a ridiculous notion if you think about it." I said this partially to get her dander up and partially because it was somewhat true. I wasn't wrestling so much with the fact of God so much as I was with the nature of God.

"Good," she said without missing a beat. This was not what I had expected. With wisdom that could be spoken only by a woman who kneaded her own bread and sewed patches over the worn-out knees of a little boy's jeans, she continued, "those with the deepest faith wrestle with the deepest doubts."

Those with the deepest faith wrestle with the deepest doubts. A paradox. Diabolical. I was sixteen and had just been trumped by a five-foot-two middle-aged woman with steamed-up bifocals. There was no argument. All I could do was seek understanding. How could it be so? Doesn't faith mean the eradication of doubt? Isn't doubt a sign of weak faith?

Eventually I would learn the wisdom in this contradiction. Those with the deepest faith get there by doggedly chasing the questions and pursuing the conflict. Doubt, conflict and debate are not contrary to faith. They are often avenues to faith. In fact, conflict is a part of faith. When we ponder an infinite God while living a finite life, we're going to feel conflicted. When we profess belief in a God who is love while living in a world governed by fear, we're going to feel conflicted. When we value selflessness but reward selfishness; when we celebrate communion but pursue elitism; when we ask God for mercy while we judge one another; when we give to the poor while exploiting cheap labor; and when we pray for peace while waging war, we're going to feel conflicted. You can't have faith without conflict. Not real faith. Not deep, meaningful faith.

Those with the deepest faith do not run from questions and conflicts, they run at them. In fact, those with the deepest faith ignite questions and conflicts.

After teaching high school religious education classes for many years, I discovered that the kids who debated and challenged everything I threw at them always ended up with a more profound spirituality than the ones who simply sat there without ever questioning. Why? Because they engaged. They sought a deeper understanding and they refused to accept superficial platitudes.

This is the gauntlet the gospel drops before us. Are we passionate enough about what we profess to believe...passionate enough to wrestle through questions and conflicts? Or do we passively walk through the motions, avoiding the difficult questions that confront us, keeping our faith in a neat, tidy box?

The choice belongs to each of us. But the cross shows us in a pretty straightforward way that serious Christianity is messy business. It's not meant to be in a neat and tidy box. You can't have true faith without conflict. And those with the deepest faith wrestle with the deepest doubts.

"POTATO-DRAINING WISDOM" FROM **GOD PLAYS A PURPLE BANJO**

WE ARE PEOPLE OF STORY. Always have been. Likely always will be. Unless we become people of video games, which is emerging as a distinct possibility. But even video games have evolved into story lines. Whether we're talking about ancient cultures gathered around the community fire in a kiva or contemporary fishermen crowded in a Northwoods bar after coming off the lake, we relate to each other through stories. We are attracted to good stories like moths to light.

Invariably, the best speakers, writers, and leaders are great storytellers. We need look no further than Jesus himself, who was a grandmaster yarn-spinner. In fact, when opening up the gospels with high school students, I often suggest we set religion and theology aside and consider Jesus as a storytelling philosopher. Once otherwise skeptical students engage with the profound insights expressed through his simple, but layered, parables, their eyes are opened to religion in new ways. Start with story, you engage them; start with religion, you lose them. Who would have thought? Well, apparently Jesus did, because that's exactly how he taught.

A good story expresses complex and abstract ideas in simple, easy-to-understand ways that are both relatable and memorable. It makes the conceptual concrete and the esoteric accessible. You can have the greatest, most compelling insight in the history of humankind, but it's not going to live beyond the boundaries of your own brain if you are unable to serve it to people in a way that is tangible, applicable, and illustrative. The story makes it stick.

I was speaking recently to a group of businesspeople about the relationship between homelessness and trauma history. The title of my presentation was "The Dark Truth of Which None Dares Speak," and it expanded on the reality that nearly every single person who is homeless has a history as an abuse victim. Admittedly, this is a bit of an abstraction for most people. Unless you've directly experienced it either as a homeless person yourself or as a pastoral minister or social worker working with those who are homeless, you're not going to relate. The last time I had given this presentation, I was speaking to a group of healthcare professionals, so I had front-loaded it with research and data. That particular audience needed to know that what I was about to share was supported by many credible studies, that it wasn't just my own personal observations and opinions. However, I goofed. I did not reshuffle my deck for the business audience.

Corporate America, I had reasoned, loves colorful charts and graphs. (This is actually ridiculously true, to the point of dangerously objectifying human beings as data points, but that's a conversation for a different day.) So I led with the data and watched as faces winced, eyes rolled, and upper lips twitched. Yikes! I was in trouble. Quickly, I realized my well-researched statistics and brilliantly articulated conclusions were flightless birds. They simply weren't getting off the ground. So I pivoted to a story about Rachel, a young woman I had met on the local streets a few years prior. Rachel had been born to a drug-addicted mother, had been introduced to drugs herself at the age of five by her mom's boyfriend at the time, and had been trafficked at the age of nine to support her mom's drug habit. Rachel was real, she was local, and she put a human name and story to my topic. The story of my personal encounter with her also gave me street cred.

Immediately, the level of engagement in the room flipped 180 degrees. People leaned forward and cocked their heads. They began asking questions and wanting more. So I told another story about Leon, and another about Judy, and another and another. For the record, whenever I tell these stories, I protect and respect identities by changing names, details and circumstance, and sometimes even age and gender to make sure the story, while still very real, cannot be traced back to any specific person. By the time I left, that particular group had decided to adopt a local school in an at-risk neighborhood, pledging financial and personal support. The stories illustrated the need for their involvement and motivated their action.

Let's look at five turbo-charging benefits a well-crafted story brings to a homily or any other presentation for that matter, and in the next chapter we'll walk through the process of how to assemble the building blocks of a good, compelling story.

1. Provides an Objective View of Self

Recall the story where God sends Nathan to King David? He has to speak truth to power. Being intuitive, he is prepared for the likelihood that David will respond defensively, perhaps even aggressively. The afflicted may appreciate being comforted, but the comfortable do not appreciate being afflicted. Not one bit. And Nathan is charged with dumping a big ol' pot of boiling affliction into the king's lap. So he tells a story about someone else—a rich man who slaughters a poor man's single, beloved lamb. David is able to objectively see the injustice, at which point Nathan is able to pull back the curtain.

Even Christians have egos. Actually, churchgoing Christians sometimes have the most confidently self-righteous egos. We teach that humility is a virtue, and we need to keep teaching it because some of us really struggle to learn it, myself included. After all, we are all legends in our own minds, and we have the inner dialog to back it up: *Sure, we're not perfect, but come on, we're working our way there, and clearly, we're smarter and more morally advanced than the soulless neighbors across the street who have the political sign in their lawn for a candidate who is the very personification of evil. They are the problem. Certainly, the problem is not me. I represent the solution. I'm a Christian, which you can tell by the*

Jesus fish on the back of my car. This whole world is going to hell in a handbasket and its only hope is for people to think, act, and believe more like I do. Sound familiar?

If you haven't had this exact conversation with parishioners, nearly verbatim, then you've certainly had it in your own head. Go ahead, admit it. We're friends here. It's safe. I'll admit it. I can feel so much better about myself when I focus on the flaws, failings, and sins of others rather than my own. And, as a homilist, one of the greatest dangers I need to protect against is the temptation to project that attitude into my homilies. It does not channel the humble love of the itinerant preacher who compassionately sat and spoke with a Samaritan woman at a noontime well.

It's one thing to be humble alongside God, but another thing entirely to be humble alongside the purple-haired kid with the neck tattoo who bags our groceries. Our ego, our self-affirming image, gets defensive real fast when someone suggests, well, maybe, hmmm, perhaps the problem is *me*.

Stories are amazing tools for opening people up to self-objectivity. They disarm defense mechanisms such as projection and downward moral comparison—that's the ego-preserving strategy whereby we admit that while we're not perfect, at least we're not as bad as *those people*. Because a well-told, relatable story is about someone other than the listener, people are able to see and understand the point, and then reflect it back onto themselves. Like David did. This process enables them to own the conclusion.

PRO-TIP FOR PREACHERS, TEACHERS, AND SOUL-REACHERS
Your listeners are far more likely to embrace a conclusion they reach themselves.

2. Establishes Ground for Commonality

Within the context of Mass, the homily carries the responsibility of reflecting on the Scriptures and pointing toward the Eucharist. OK, that's probably the most "churchy" thing you'll read in this book. It's certainly among the most "churchy" things I've ever written. In my booklet *How to Talk Catholic and Still Get Lunch Invitations*, I caution that religiously high-brow language can be off-putting for a lot of people. The same holds true, by the way, in homilies. People will relate to the message far more readily if it's offered in language that's comfortable and accessible for them. But if you're reading this particular book, I think you can handle it, so I use it here because it is crisp and true. The homily connects our common story (Scripture) with our Communion table and prepares us to take the wholeness of this reality back out into the broader community.

Common story, Communion table, broader community. You see the common thread?

There's a lot packed in there and I'll leave it to the liturgists and theologians to break it all open and debate what it means. But for the folks sitting in the pews, it means this: help me grow ever more closely toward unity with God and creation so that I can better love God with all my heart, mind, and soul and more authentically love my neighbor as myself. That's it. On a deep spiritual plane, this is what gives life meaning and that's what people hunger for.

Intellectually, people coming to church or streaming online know the Scriptures convey the sacred wisdom of the ages, but they struggle to unpack them and relate them to their own life experience. A good story can do that. Likewise, they know Eucharist is the real presence of Christ, but they seek a more profound understanding of how to let it transform them. A good story can do that, too. And they know they will find peace when they apply all of this to their lives and their relationships, but they're looking for insights on how to do that beyond a few easy, broad brush strokes. Again, this is what good stories do.

Relatable stories bring it all together in three ways: First, they help people see that their own life journey is, in fact, the human journey passed through time. Second, stories help make real the idea that Eucharist is not merely an object: it's a shared encounter and a lived experience. And third, stories illustrate how (or how not) to find wholeness and happiness by living it all out.

> PRO-TIP FOR PREACHERS, TEACHERS, AND SOUL-REACHERS
> **If your message drives more division than unity, you whiffed. I've learned this one the hard way.**

3. Make the Abstract Tangible and Applicable

I opened this chapter with a story titled "Potato-Draining Wisdom" from *God Plays a Purple Banjo*, which was derived from the text of a homily I gave a few years ago. The topic was the symbiotic relationship between faith and doubt. Pardon my abruptness, but holy hell! That's about as conceptual as it gets. As part of everyone's human experience, the relationship between faith and doubt stirs inner conflict and causes us to question the very existence of God. We need to talk about it. But we don't know how. It's too much like holding stardust in our hands. It's real and wondrous, but we can't quite get a grasp on it. Also, we worry that it's radioactive.

Well-told stories take big ideas like this, ideas that have sun-like potential to nurture spiritual growth, and frame them in a way we can touch, feel, and experience. Consider, for example, the story of the prodigal son. I mean, holy cow! Is that not the gourmet bacon-mac & cheese of all stories ever told? It takes gigantic, deep truths and serves them by the forkful so we can taste, chew, and digest the profound richness.

Now, while the prodigal son might be the gold standard of how to express abstractions through relatable stories, most of us mere mortals will freeze like deer in the headlights if we measure our own stories against it. So take the pressure off yourself. Reflect on your own life experiences and encounters. Certainly, you have intersected with deep truth. Tell the real-world stories you've stumbled on, tripped over, and perhaps have been bulldozed by. A real story, however simple, is far more accessible to listeners than a grand story you make up. Again, the story of an exchange with my mother at the beginning of this chapter is a tangible illustration of that.

For the record, many biblical historians suggest the prodigal son story was at least somewhat autobiographical. If that's so, then even Jesus drew stories from his own experience and did not try to make them up out of thin air.

PRO-TIP FOR PREACHERS, TEACHERS, AND SOUL-REACHERS
The most effective stories are taken straight from the grit of human experience. They make the abstract accessible because the stories themselves are accessible and relatable.

4. Engage in a Memorable Way

A woman pulled her lawn chair alongside mine on the sideline of a youth soccer game and got right to the point. "Hi, I'm Alicia. My son, Alec, plays for De Pere."

I was surprised and caught off guard. Parents usually cluster with their own kind, so to speak. My son played for her son's archrival. What was going on? What sort of radical gash was she trying to tear into the social fabric? Still, I had long been of the disposition that youth soccer is nothing more than a bunch of kids kicking a ball around in the park, and parents give it far more gravitas than it deserves. So I shook off my perplexity and expressed delight at making the acquaintance. "Güten tag, Frau Alicia. Setzin Sie hier, bitte. Es ist ein schöner tag!" I always speak German when I'd rather be left alone.

No, of course that's not what I did! I happily engaged, "Hi, Alicia, I'm S—"

"Oh, I know who you are," she cut me off. I guess the German thing wouldn't have worked anyway. "You're the deacon at St. Elizabeth Seton. That's why I sat down here."

Great, I thought. I just wanted to relax, page through some *New Yorker* magazines (for the cartoons—let's not kid ourselves), and watch a little soccer. The last thing I wanted to do was engage in a conversation about religion.

She continued, "I was at your church a few years ago and you gave a homily that really changed my whole life. It opened me up and completely changed the way I see things. It changed the way I relate to my children, and it really changed the way I treat my husband. We were going through a rough time and your homily probably saved our marriage. When I saw you here, I just needed to come over and thank you."

"That's very kind," I said. "Thank you. It's really good to know something I put out there actually landed. Of course, now I have to ask...what on earth did I say? Perhaps I need to listen to it myself."

She then relayed a story I had told about a conversation with one of my sons when he backed one of my cars out of the garage and scraped it alongside another of my cars that was sitting in the driveway. Oh, yes. I remembered.

PRO-TIP FOR PREACHERS, TEACHERS, AND SOUL-REACHERS
Stories stick. Alicia didn't remember exactly when it happened or even why she was visiting my church that day, but she remembered the story and the person who told it. For thousands of years, this is how cultures passed their truths from one generation to another. Stories make things both memorable and re-tellable.

5. Navigate Emotions

The human brain is a freaky miracle. We're talking about one hundred billion neurons packed together in a three-pound ball that's seventy-five percent water. If you study it, it'll blow your hair off. It might be the most amazing, high-powered component in all creation, even when it's not functioning very well, which happens when it's overrun with teenage hormones, doused with alcohol, or elected to Congress. In fairness, lightning storms are arguably even more high-powered than the brain, but they lack the ability to control, process, or network, so what good is all that power?

Here's a little something worth remembering: your listeners all have reasonably well-functioning brains. Mostly. You might question that due to all the blank stares they give you, but I'm going to ask you to trust me on this. They think, ponder, imagine, dream, worry, grieve, question, and do all of the other wonderful things human brains do. They also work independently of your brain. Gasp, right? As you speak, they don't automatically follow. They do their own thing.

But here is what they do follow: emotions. Every single time. Inevitably. This is a truth every bit as reliable as death, taxes, and the shelf-life of Twinkies. Thinking follows emotions. We feel things before we think about them. This is how the brain is wired. You can throw an idea out to your listeners, and it absolutely must pass through the tinted filters of emotion before it reaches the parts of the brain that objectively consider and analyze. I once commented in a homily about disliking tomatoes and received a visceral reaction from the tomato lovers that rivaled the emotional blow-back I received from speaking on the morality of immigration policy. If you're looking at the state of our western culture and wondering why no one seems able to have a rational, objective conversation about anything, it's because everything gets hung up in the emotional filters. Once an idea is stuck there, it can't get out.

By the way, I believe boredom is an emotion. If you incite boredom in your listeners, whatever point you're throwing out there is not going to land.

Stories have a magical way of weaving through the politics of the brain. Listeners relax and let their guards down. Time stands still. As long as the story isn't about them, it's not threatening. When we settle into a good story, we leave ourselves for a couple of minutes and enter the world of someone else, thereby opening ourselves to empathy. We let ourselves actually feel and process these emotions so the story's point or moral can actually be received objectively into the parts of the brain where we can think about it. This is what happened when Nathan told the story to David. Had he started with, "So, uhm, yeah...let's talk about the injustice of adultery," his point never would have gotten through and he never would have gotten out of there with his head still attached.

PRO-TIP FOR PREACHERS, TEACHERS, AND SOUL-REACHERS
If you can't navigate the emotions evoked by your point, you won't be able to control your own narrative. A good story is an outstanding device for helping your point weave through your listeners' emotional jungle.

A Few Things Worth Hanging On To

- A good story expresses complex and abstract ideas in simple, easy-to-understand ways that are both relatable and memorable. It makes the conceptual concrete and the esoteric accessible.

- Stories crash through ego defenses and enable people to safely reflect objectively on themselves.

- We are ultimately all part of something far bigger than ourselves; we are people of community. A well-told story connects us with each other across the pews, across the social-political spectrum, and even across time.

- The best stories are real and tangible, taken from the grit of human experience.

- We remember and share stories, so they resonate with listeners in a way that can be carried forward and passed along.

- The human brain is wired to respond emotively before responding rationally. A compelling story is able to navigate the complex emotional filters within your listeners so it can get through and be processed and considered.

How to Build a Good Story

I had a real come-to-Jesus moment on my way to church one Sunday morning. It rattled me. I was approaching the stop sign on LaCount, a quiet tree-lined street on normal days but really sleepy on Sunday mornings, when a white car flew by on West Point Avenue. Right after it disappeared from the angle of my view, I heard a loud BOOM, an awful scraping sound, and a smashing crash. I reached the intersection and looked to the west. The car was upside down in the east bound lane with half of a utility pole laying alongside. The other half of the pole was suspended above, bouncing in place like a puppet on wires.

Thoughts raced through my mind. Do I turn right and go offer whatever assistance I can? Or do I turn left and continue on to church? This should be a no-brainer, but I froze for just a moment. I didn't actually see the accident, so I wasn't a witness, and

I was already running late. People would be congregating and Fr. Willie would not have prepared a homily, so I had an obligation to get to Mass. Also, in a rebellion against technology, I had been practicing phone-free Sundays, so I wasn't able to call 911 to report the crash or call the church to tell them I'd be late. I turned right and raced a block up to the accident. What's the point of church, I thought, if we don't reach out to our brothers and sisters in need?

LET'S HIT THE PAUSE BUTTON RIGHT THERE. There's a lot more to the story, of course, and you're likely on the edge of your seat with bated breath as you wonder what happened next. Maybe we'll get to that a bit later if you eat all the vegetables I'm scooping onto your plate first. All of the building blocks of a complete story are in the two paragraphs above. You might remember them from middle school English, but let's unpack and review them anyway, just in case thirteen-year-old you was preoccupied with, well, the natural insecurities and curiosities of thirteen-year-old you.

Setting

We are visual people, even, perhaps especially, in our minds. It is so much easier for your listeners to enter the story you're telling if they can place themselves there. So give them a little reference. In this case, it's a quiet tree-lined street in a residential neighborhood near the church. That's probably enough. If you're writing a novel, you can expand for pages on the poetry of crimson maple leaves in crisp autumn air, layering in a nested reflection on the circle of life. You can wax on about the irony of the utility service truck parked in a neighbor's driveway, while the unaware young service technician still slept next to his pregnant wife. In twenty minutes, he would be awoken by a page telling him to step outside and get to work.

When telling stories, people tend to gloss over the setting entirely by ignoring it or being overly generic, or they go all Moby Dick on the details. The brief story above would have been rendered less relatable if I had jumped straight into plot: *I was approaching a stop sign when a white car flew buy on the crossroad.* Admittedly, this would not have changed the story's message or point in a meaningful way, but it would have been more difficult for the listener to enter the story and place themselves there. Setting makes the story more accessible, engaging, and memorable.

Remember, the purpose of your story is to make a point that resonates with your listeners. Give just a couple of details to establish the setting, but don't bury them there.

Character

Character makes or breaks the deal. Straight up. Stories are like life in general this way. It's probably worthwhile to distinguish between character as a noun and character as an attribute. When telling a story, you'll want your noun to have attributes just like you want your beer to have taste. It's what makes people real. For example, the author of this book is a middle-aged guy in the upper Midwest. Boring. The author of this book is a fifty-six-year old deacon man-child who swaps *Mad Magazines* with homeless people. Now we have a noun with attributes, a character with character. You want to know this guy. In fact, you probably want to donate money to his favorite charity.

Characters with character make your story human and accessible. It's really how your listeners relate to the story and understand that what your characters experience is also what they experience personally. All of Scripture has survived for thousands of years because people were characters with character. I mean, look at Job. Who among us hasn't identified with that little dude from time to time?

So, here are a few pointers:

1. Start with the central conflict and do not get derailed or distracted by characters not germane to that conflict. The brief story at the beginning of this chapter expresses an inner conflict, man vs. self, so the only character needing attention is the person who is having the conflict; in this case it was me. The story at the beginning of the last chapter was a man vs. God conflict, so it needed only two characters, myself and a wisdom figure who was personified in my mother. I did not add my brother, sister, or father to the story. While their presence might have added texture, they would have been distracting and would have unnecessarily lengthened the story.

2. Limit the number of characters to as few as necessary, preferably one or two, but never more than three. Seriously, you're telling a brief story to help illustrate a point and make it relatable; you're not writing *Game of Thrones*. Someone else already did that and it ended badly. When Jesus told the story of the prodigal son and his brother, he masterfully layered two conflicts: man vs. God and man vs. man, but even

at that he only needed three characters. That's the most your listeners can keep track of.

3. Make your characters real. When you tell a story, tell it about real people dealing with the demands and conflicts of real life. There is always a temptation to create two-dimensional characters that simplify good and evil. Life isn't really like that in the world beyond George Lucas' *Star Wars* universe, which, while offering great mythological insights, is nonetheless fictional. In reality, we're all saints and we're all sinners, and we spend most of our lives working to be more of one and less of the other. After reading one of my short stories aloud in class, my Advanced Creative Writing professor, the brilliant Bruce Taylor, asked me if I liked one of the characters. When I responded that I did not, he publicly chastised, "How dare you? How dare you create this character, saddle him with negative attributes, and then dislike him for it? You created him that way!" The point, which sent me to a local bar after class, hit home. When preaching, teaching, or soul-reaching, never tell a story about a character you don't like. As the narrator of the story, you need to be a role model of love and mercy.

Trajectory or Story Arc

One of the most frequent comments I receive after Mass is this: "You know, you started out with that story and I was thinking to myself, 'where is he going with this?'" I secretly light up inside when I hear that. Attention had been captured. People cannot resist a good story that places a strong character on a compelling arc. We want to follow them and find out what happens. It's often the difference between a ten-minute homily that feels like four minutes, and a five-minute homily that feels like twenty minutes. When you give people a story with an irresistible trajectory, time stands still.

Harkening back to the master, Jesus brilliantly held the focused minds of his listeners by controlling the story arc. Consider the parable of the servant who buries the talents his master entrusted to his stewardship, or the parable of the vineyard owner who kept hiring people throughout the day and then paid them all the same. We listen and pay attention because we want to see how it unfolds.

Traditionally, this component of storytelling was referred to as plot, but over the last couple of decades the term *trajectory* has been increasingly preferred. While *plot* has the potential to be stagnant, *trajectory* implies movement or journey. Something has to happen; the story needs to move forward. As a bonus to this evolution in terminology, you can sound way cooler when you talk about movies with your friends. "The film's trajectory had an irresistible arc, although it plateaued during that predictable love scene," makes you sound a whole lot more interesting as a human being than, "Dude, I liked the plot."

There are two big watch-outs that can swirl you into storytelling quicksand. The first is when a trajectory is allowed to meander, take detours, and get side-tracked. Again, if you're writing a novel, you can afford to incorporate all sorts of devices such as nested stories, flashbacks, subplots, and sidebars. These are all essentially stories layered within stories, component parts that contribute to the larger story. But you're not writing a novel; you're telling a story that illustrates a larger point in six to eight minutes. Keep your trajectory singular and directional.

The second watch-out has to do with the scope of the trajectory. Keep it simple. You're not writing the *Iliad*. At the beginning of this chapter, I shared a story with a trajectory that in real time took about ten seconds. That's it. It's all I needed to set up and illustrate the timeless point being advanced. I left off the front end of the story that got me to the intersection, and the back end about what happened when I arrived on the scene of the accident. Those are, in effect, their own stories worth saving for another time. Likewise in "Potato-Draining Wisdom," the story opening the last chapter. The story arc is very simple and contained, merely a momentary exchange between a boy and his mother.

Before getting to the final building blocks of story—authenticity, emotion, and hook—let's take a break for another story. This is a story called "Jeremiah" from my book *Jesus Wears Socks with Sandals*. The conflict is man vs. society. See if you can identify the setting, the two main characters, and the trajectory.

JEREMIAH

A scrawny wisp of a ten-year-old boy came wheeling up to our StreetLights Outreach Block Party on a bicycle with only one pedal. He would push down as hard as he could with his right foot, trying to create enough momentum to crank the pedal 360 degrees, and then sort of push along with his left foot. His name was Jeremiah, and I swore that if you stacked the letters of his name on edge, they'd be taller than he was. At first he was a little shy, refusing the hamburger I offered because he didn't have any money. But once I told him the burgers were free, he gladly devoured one, and then another. And another. This little kid pounded away six hamburgers, several mountains of potato chips, and I have no idea how many cookies. Then he shoved a handful of cookies into the pockets of his sweatshirt and said he was going to go tell his brothers and sisters to come over to the park and get something to eat because, he said, "we never eat like this at home."

"You never get hamburgers at home?" I asked mostly as a form of active listening. I knew how it was for many of the kids in this neighborhood. They ate breakfast and lunch at school, and then dinner was a bit of a craps shoot. But this was July. There was no school.

"No," he said. That wasn't what he meant, so he clarified, "We never get to eat until we're not hungry anymore."

Go ahead and let that steep in your tea for a moment.

Most of us have the privilege of eating until we're full, and many of us keep expanding that capacity. We even joke about it as we age, patting our increased girth with self-deprecating pride. But standing before me in the wealthiest nation in human history was a kid who wasn't talking about eating until he's full. He was talking about never being able to eat until the hunger went away. This is what I do between meals! I snack to make the hunger go away. Could it be, I wondered, that I snack as much or even more than Jeremiah and his siblings eat all day?

While all this was going on, a couple of our Spokes of Hope volunteers fixed his bike and gave it a second pedal. As he rode off, Jeremiah was an entirely transformed kid, exploding with hope, excitement, and unquenchable energy. When he returned about twenty minutes later, he had four sisters and two brothers with him; all were wide-eyed. Then he raced off again to tell some friends and cousins.

In the meantime, his mother showed up to check it out. Her presence anchored the children and they swarmed our serving lines like a hive of bees with its queen. When we were done for the evening, we packed up all the leftover hamburgers, hotdogs, buns, chips, cookies, and sodas, and we gave it all to her. As her caravan of kids left the park, each loaded with a bag or box full of food, she could be heard saying over and over, "Praise Jesus, praise Jesus, praise Jesus," as tears rolled down her cheeks.

For me, this was a resurrection moment. You see, when the Romans crucified Jesus, they didn't just want to kill him, they wanted to kill his entire message and his movement. They wanted to kill hope. To preserve their own power and privilege, they wanted to kill his ideas about human value and dignity. They saw these as dangerous notions. So when Jesus rises from the dead, the entire body of his work, his teaching, rises with him. Love of God and love of neighbor rises to new life. Matthew 25—what you do for the least, you do for me—rises from the tomb. The beatitudes—blessed are the poor in spirit—the compassion of the good Samaritan, the dignity of the leper, the forgiveness and mercy revealed in the parable of the prodigal son, the value of the woman at the well, and the hope of the Centurion whose servant was ill... it all rises to new life, the exact same new life expressed by the woman and her children in the park. Praise Jesus.

Two thousand year later, we're still living out that resurrection. Every time we spread love into the world, every time we feed the hungry, comfort the sick, welcome the stranger, we are giving flesh, blood, and breath to the living Christ. We aren't just celebrating resurrection; we BECOME resurrection. And that should fill us with joy until we're stuffed full, with enough extra to shove it in our pockets to carry to others.

This story, by the way, was originally written and offered as an Easter homily. The church was packed to capacity with nearly a thousand people of all ages and spiritual dispositions. Take a step back and think about that for a minute. There are times when the people sitting in the pews are not like-minded, when they come from different places geographically, experientially, spiritually, and even theologically. How on earth do you speak with compelling relevancy to such a sea of diversity? Story. This is why Jesus used so may stories in his preaching, teaching, and soul-reaching. A well-told story provides a common experience and reference for listeners; it becomes glue that unites us together.

Authenticity

An artificial religion is of little use in the real world. It's like staying at the Venetian in Las Vegas and thinking you're in Italy because you see gondolas in canals and hear someone playing an accordion in the background. I once overheard a conversation in a coffee shop in which a woman said, "There is really no need to go to Europe. Just go to Epcot. It's exactly the same thing." I wanted to scream NO! and the Rainforest Café is not the Amazon.

The real world is not covered with a sanitized, disinfected coat of paint. It's textured with grit. People laugh and cry, marriages succeed and fail, healthy people get cancer, the neighbor's cat doogies in your daughter's sandbox. Life is a mess! Arguably, it's often a delightfully life-giving mess like a kindergarten classroom on fingerpainting day, but it can also feel like the mess of an urban battlefield. This is the world Jesus lived in and told stories about. Sometimes the seeds you spread with the best intentions fall on the footpath, and the birds come and eat them and digest them and then redeposit them on your windshield. Such is the way of things.

A good story is not just for the world; it's of the world. Rather than make it up, simply pay attention. Stories are happening and unfolding around you all the time. If you look around and see no stories that reveal profound truths about the human experience, then you're living in the Venetian rather than Venice. Go sit in a bus stop for half an hour. Walk into a bowling alley on a Friday night. Immerse yourself in humanity. Jesus will show up, I promise. Humanity is where he hangs out.

When coaching writers, I remind them that creation is a big place where remarkable things happen, but the distance between their own ears is only about six inches. If they try to create their stories, they are limited to very narrow real estate. A good writer recognizes and captures real stories in a real world; he doesn't try to invent them. When Monet painted *The Water Lily Pond*, he used a real pond for reference. He may have embellished and made the colors richer and the fauna denser. That's his right as the artist. Heck, he could have added a frog or a kid fishing off the bridge if he wanted. That would have been perfectly acceptable. The point is that the story he told with his painting is based in reality. When you tell stories in homilies or presentations, and I sure hope you do, you are free to add dimension and even characters, but base it all in reality. In this way, your stories will be authentic and true to life itself, and the listener will be able to relate to them.

Emotion

We've already discussed a fair amount about the importance of emotion in a homily. It's worth noting, however, that effectively conveying emotion through a story you're telling is a little trickier than the other elements we've already discussed. Your words certainly matter, but your delivery matters even more. A lot more, actually.

Here's the deal: we are wired to read emotions from facial cues, body language, and voice tone. You can mute a movie's volume and fully understand the emotions without hearing a word or knowing anything about the story trajectory. Mountains of research have been done on this. I always thought it'd be keen to study the faces of people watching movies without sound. I wonder if their own facial expressions and posture mirror the emotions conveyed in the movie.

> PRO-TIP FOR PREACHERS, TEACHERS, AND SOUL-REACHERS
> **Pepper in surprising and quirky words once in a while. They tickle people. You probably noticed I used the word "keen" in the previous paragraph. In fact, you likely went back and read over it a second time. Originally, I had used the word "amazing," but I changed it to "keen" because I love you too much to saddle you with tired language all the time.**

Back to the point. When telling a story, you need to be a bit of an actor. Your facial expressions, body language, and voice tone should convey the emotions of the story. It's also worthwhile to add in details about the nonverbal cues of the characters in your story. Recall the story of the woman caught in adultery. The author of John's gospel adds in this compelling detail about Jesus stooping down and writing in the dirt with his finger. When they demanded an answer, he stood up and delivered the famous line about casting the first stone. Then the gospel's author has him stoop down again and write in the dust. Jesus' body language adds layers of emotion to the story. Jesus tells an entire story, conveying layers of calming, contemplative emotion simply through his body language.

A Hook

As each of my three sons approached the age of thirteen, he reminded me of a critical life lesson: I am not, by default, worth listening to. Shocking. Each time I relearned this, I was as surprised by it as you are. In my head, I am a wise sage in a flannel shirt, like a cowboy poet. Apparently, they inherited a selective attention gene from their mother. Whatever would come out of my mouth was not nearly as attention-worthy as whatever was already in their minds.

ME: I want to give you some life-shaping insight passed down to me from the fires of generations that went before...

ANY OF MY THREE SONS: (crickets)

ME: I think this will help you with the anxiety you feel about school, homework, and your path to future happiness and personal fulfillment.

ANY OF MY THREE SONS: (yawn)

ME: YOUR MOTHER AND I HAVE SOLD YOU TO A THIRD-WORLD MILITIA!!

ANY OF MY THREE SONS: Do we have any food in this house?

Perhaps the single biggest mistake preachers and other public speakers make is that they assume people are listening simply because they are talking. I promise you they are not. Attention must be earned. I'm going to say that again in case your mind had wandered off with a bag of cheesy Doritos and you were dreaming about being on *Family Feud*. Attention must be earned.

It is widely estimated that Americans are now exposed to over 10,000 marketing messages a day. Think about that. If you sleep for eight hours a day, that equates to 10.4 messages every waking minute. That's insane! The average adult takes between twelve and twenty breaths per minute, which means someone is trying to capture our mind's attention nearly as often as we breathe! Whoa! Maybe you have an IBM Watson type of superpower enabling you to process this incessant pelting of mostly uninvited banality, but most of us do not. Instead, we have trained our minds to screen and triage all the noise. We filter it before it even gets inside our heads, letting in only that which is worthwhile to us.

The first layer of this filter is intrigue. The second layer is relevancy, which we have discussed at length already. But before your words can even get to the relevancy filter, they have to first pass through the highly selective filter of intrigue. Without even thinking about it, we ask ourselves this very simple question: Is there anything about this that might be worth an investment of my attention? Does it offer potential for me to laugh, grow, cry, discover, or understand something new? Might it enrich me in any way?

It's probably worth emphasizing that this is not personal. Your listeners' minds have been trained on a subconscious level to tune out almost all messages that fly at them. If they didn't, their heads would explode like the crystal skulls at the end of the fourth Indiana Jones movie, and they'd be destined to a fried-brain life as reality television stars. As soon as you start speaking, they automatically activate the intrigue filter and you have to earn your way through. If you smile, they might give you a second shot at passing through. If they know you and like you, they might even give you a third chance, but don't count on it. Sometimes those who are most familiar with us are the quickest to dismiss us.

Think of a story's hook as the device that opens passage through the intrigue filter. It could be a statement that conveys urgency or mystery. Or the promise of a payoff. It's the on-ramp to the story, causing your listeners to engage with "what's coming next" curiosity. This chapter opened with a story using the simple and inexpensive hook, "I had a real come-to-Jesus moment on the way to church one morning." With this hook, I achieved the following:

- Created curiosity—What happened?

- Identified whose story it was—my own.

- Introduced setting—the community was familiar with the church neighborhood.

The way I delivered the hook introduced tone and gravitas. If I had spilled coffee on my tan pants and wrestled with the question about whether to rush home and change, I might have used the same words as a hook, but I would have spoken them with a lighter voice and wry smile. But this hook was setting up a more serious situation and a more existential question—what's my faith really about? So my tone was slower and more introspective: *I had, uhmm...I had a real come-to-Jesus moment on the way to church one morning. It rattled me.*

OK, you've finished all the vegetables. I'll complete the story. How many meaningful, relevant homilies are in this one narrative?

As I sprang from my truck and mounted a middle-aged sprint toward the scene, the driver of the overturned car crawled out of the passenger's window and scrambled on hands and knees away from the wreck. The neighbors stood with gaping mouths, physically frozen as my mind had been just a moment ago.

"Call 911! Call 911!" I called to the neighbors. No one seemed to move. I ran to the guy who had emerged from the car and was now on his feet walking in confused, wandering circles. I approached him as calmly as I could, angling to square with his unshaven but surprisingly unmarred face so I could see into his eyes. They appeared distant, disconnected from the moment's time and space.

I, too, was lost and confused. I had no training in crisis mitigation or trauma intervention. They don't teach that in deacon school and I had no idea what to do. A guy on the sidewalk hollered out, "I think he blew a tire and it flipped the car."

Again, I called to the neighbors standing in the driveway, "Has anyone called 911? Please call 911!"

"Oh, yeah," replied a bearded man as he fished a phone from the pocket of his pajama pants. He handed it to the young woman standing alongside him, "Here, you do it. I don't know what to say."

The guy who was in the car continued walking in circles and I found myself walking alongside him. "My name is Steve," I said. "What's your name?"

"Alex. Oh, my God, my mom is going to kill me."

"Alex," I said, "you're OK. Right now, you're OK." I had no idea if this was the right thing or the wrong thing to say. My instincts just said this is what he needed to hear. So it's what I said.

"My mom is going to kill me. That's her car. Oh, my God."

"Your mom is going to be grateful that you're OK, Alex. She loves you more than the car."

"My mom lives just a few blocks from here. I'm on my way to her house. That's her car. I wrecked her car."

Again, the guy on the sidewalk blurted out, "I think he blew a tire and it flipped the car. Yup, I heard a boom before the crash. That's what probably happened."

I heard sirens approaching. Help was on the way. I placed one of my hands on each of Alex's shoulders and looked into his eyes again. "The car isn't important, Alex. You are. Would you like me to pray with you?" He nodded, so we stood there and prayed together until the first responders arrived.

A Few Things Worth Hanging On To

- Establish your story's setting in a simple way that anchors listeners in a context they can visualize.

- When telling stories, make your characters real. Give them names and an identifiable detail your listeners can picture. Also, use only one or two main characters, never more three.

- Keep your story's trajectory simple and controlled. Stay focused.

- Your audience will best relate to real stories from the real world. Don't try to make them up. Instead, simply capture them in the wild and bring them into the church.

- Attention must be earned, so be deliberate about your story's hook. It's so much easier to draw people in at the beginning than to win them over along the way.

Why Humor Helps

SHAKESPEARE WAS A COMEDIAN. STRAIGHT UP. Dude was a riot, a sixteenth-century Seinfeld on laughing gas. When most of us study Shakespeare in high school, we're too intimidated in our effort to decipher the language to catch the jokes, so we miss the brilliance. Well, at least until someone explains to us how much of his humor is a bit off color and bawdy; then we perk up and pay attention—because we're fifteen and human, and that's what fifteen-year-old humans do.

We often forget that the bard who had the greatest depth of insight into the human character since Jesus himself, the writer who gave humanity the romance of *Romeo and Juliet* and the tragedy of *King Lear*, was also a comic genius. Through the character of Sir John Falstaff, who appears in three of his plays, Shakespeare basically invented the modern notion of comic relief. A lot of homilies could benefit from a little comic relief. Additionally, there is a whole branch of humor called "malapropisms," which Shakespeare leveraged to give dimension to the character of Mistress Quickly, the innkeeper in four plays. As a reminder in case you slept through the most interesting day in your sophomore English class, a malapropism is a misstatement caused by naively substituting a similar word for the intended word. Allow me to rephrase: it's when you unknowingly use the wrong word and it's funny. One of my favorite uses of a malapropism is when I respond to a friendly jab by saying, "Hey, I resemble that remark," rather than saying I resent that remark.

The question is *why?* Why did Shakespeare pepper so much humor into his writing? Clearly, he was a grand master of character development, trajectory, and authenticity. His stories conveyed brilliant insights into the human experience in ways that remain as poignant and crisp five hundred years later. In fact, some of Shakespeare's insights are so proverbial that people believe they're actually biblical (i.e., "this above all else, to thine own self be true"). So why did he joke around so much? Was it just his personality? His desire to entertain?

In his book *Laughing with God*, Gerald Arbuckle explains that the books of the Bible, including the gospels, are filled with humor. We often miss the jokes, he explains, because humor is often cultural and we are not from the same cultures as Jesus and other biblical personalities. The parables Jesus told, the stories that form a cornerstone of his teaching method, are packed with humor, Arbuckle explains. His listeners would have recognized and appreciated the comedic bent of hyperbole and incongruity.

Why would Jesus have joked around even at all? Isn't the salvation of all humankind serious business?

Arbuckle opens the very first chapter of his book with this insightful quote from Conrad Hyers: "If humor without faith is in danger of dissolving into cynicism and despair, faith without humor is in danger of turning into arrogance and intolerance." Hmmm...arrogance and intolerance...have you ever come across Christians who never laugh? They tend to be a rather judgmental lot, wouldn't you say? Hyers is on to something. When speaking before various groups, I like to gauge the religious temperament of the audience, so I often seed this little gem early in my presentation: "I've learned you have to be careful of what you say about Catholicism. It's like a religion to some people." Normally, enough people chuckle at the wry incongruity of that statement, letting me know that it's OK to be human in this room. We can relax and enjoy the time together. But it's also not unusual that this remark is met with stone-cold faces. Then I know I need to watch my step because I'm dealing with a group of folks who have never given a Starbucks barista a made-up name. By the way, if ever you hear the barista call out "Esteban Diego," that's my hot chocolate.

This brings us to the first way humor helps a homily. It keeps the homilist humble and human. People relate better to humble human homilists. They perk up and open up, hoping that perhaps the subsequent message is going to be relatable and relevant. Humor says you "get" life, you understand the befuddled realities and contradictions regular people bumble through on most days.

In particular, if you can make jokes about yourself, all the better! Self-deprecating humor is a sign of emotional intelligence and is linked to psychological well-being. Go ahead and google it. You'll find all sorts of very credible articles and research. And if there are two qualities the people in the pews really want from the person standing in front dropping the word of God on them, it's these: emotional intelligence and psychological well-being. We're all carrying around enough of our own mixed-up baggage; no one wants to get buried under whatever the preacher is working through and compensating for. In a homily reflecting on our call to live as role models of love and mercy, I once referenced my wife, "If you're looking for a role model of patience and perseverance, I invite you to look no further than Michelle. I don't mean to brag, but because of me a lot of people pray for her." Boom! I won over the women by praising my wife, and I humbled myself in the process.

A second way humor helps a homily is that it bonds people together. This is a super important point. Laughter is a very social expression. It unifies people. What better way to prime a community for sharing Holy Communion than expressing joy together? Think back to the best dinners you've had in your life, the ones you remember most fondly. Sure, the conversation was compelling and the meal itself was delicious, but I'm willing to wager it was the laughter that made the most indelible mark. In fact, I'll bet the laughter actually made the conversation richer and the food taste even better. When people laugh together, they linger together. They hang out and have dessert.

Have you ever been to one of those fancy-pants charity galas or banquets—the kind where people wear uncomfortable shoes and smile at each other without creating lines in their faces? Everyone sits awkwardly around tables and makes polite conversation.

"So what brings you here this evening?"

"Oh, my wife works with someone on the planning committee. What about you?"

"My wife and I have been supporting this organization

for a number of years, so, yeah, we come back to this event every year."

"Well, they sure seem like they're doing good work in the community."

"Yes, yes, they do. There's a big need."

Uncomfortable pause.

"Hey, would you rather sneak outside, sit on the tailgate of my truck, crack open a couple of PBR's, and tell jokes about the Minnesota Vikings?"

"Absolutely, I would! But if I do, I'll have to sleep in the garage for the next three nights, so I need to keep sitting here pretending it's a really nice evening as I watch treasured minutes of my life swirl down a drain called boredom."

We've all been to these things, checking our watches by 7:45 pm and planning our getaway. If you look around the room, you'll notice fifty grown men staring at the phones they're holding under the table. They're checking basketball scores. I know because I've been among them. Getting caught is awkward.

MICHELLE: "Are you on your phone?"

ME: "Uhmmm...I'm just getting an update on the silent auction items, dear. Making sure no one has outbid you on that basket of essential oils, candles, and dried apricot potpourri."

MICHELLE: "Oh, good. Do I still have the high bid?"

ME: "Sure. I wonder how the Badgers are doing..."

GUY AT THE NEXT TABLE STARING INTO HIS LAP:
"The Badgers are ahead by seven at halftime."

Have you noticed, though, there is always at least one table at these events where people are laughing riotously and genuinely having a good time? And have you noticed that's always the last table to clear out at the end of the night? If you haven't ever observed this, it's because you've always been saddled at a boring, polite table where everyone eases toward the exits as soon as it is socially acceptable.

> PRO-TIP FOR PREACHERS, TEACHERS, AND SOUL-REACHERS
> **If you want to foster a dynamic in your community where people linger in hospitality, seed humor into your homilies.**

A third way humor helps homilies is by relaxing people and opening them up. Listeners lower their ego defenses and let their emotional guards down. Once you've given people reason to smile or even chuckle a bit, they'll let you touch their hearts. Humor helps people cross the threshold into emotional and spiritual vulnerability.

In the short term, laughter also enhances the intake of oxygen-rich air and simulates vital organs including the heart and lungs. When we laugh, more endorphins are released from the brain, and our heart and blood pressure increase a bit and then decrease. The net result of all this physiological activity is a good, relaxed feeling. Stress leaves the body. Hmmm...imagine that: people who laugh a little during a homily will thus enter Eucharist with a joyful heart and a good, relaxed feeling.

Additionally, the long-term benefits of laughter include an improved immune system, pain relief, increased personal satisfaction, and a better disposition. People who laugh are just overall happier and healthier.

The irony of this is that people really want to feel happier when they leave church than when they entered. They want to feel uplifted, comforted, or enriched in some way. Yet, they're reluctant to laugh in church. It's as though they need permission. This is a real exchange that happened after Mass:

PARISHIONER:	"Thank you for that homily. The humor was perfect."
ME:	"That's very nice to hear, thank you. I'm glad you found it enriching."
PARISHIONER:	"Your story was spot on. That's exactly how things are between me and my husband. I wanted to laugh out loud."
ME:	"So why didn't you?"
PARISHIONER:	"Why didn't I laugh out loud? Well, I didn't think it was appropriate to laugh in church."

Where in the world did this notion come from? It's not appropriate to laugh in church? It's not appropriate to express unbridled joy as we gather together around the Lord's table? Holy smokes, we can be a confused and contradictory religion. How many preachers have stood in front of a community, talking at great length about what a valuable gift human life is, but never act like a joy-filled child on Christmas morning opening that gift?

People need cues and permissions from the homilist letting them know it's OK to relax and enjoy the time they're sharing together. Here's another bonus from the world of science: if you make people laugh, they'll find you more attractive and you'll look younger. Seriously. For some of you reading this, looking younger and attractive comes naturally. But some of us need the boost. Don't judge.

We all know perpetually youthful, well-loved preachers who open every homily with a joke. They have that quality best described as being eighty but going on thirty. Bless them, but I could never do that. I don't know enough jokes, I struggle to remember jokes, and I have no idea where they find all those jokes. This is rather ironic since my children have told me many times that I am, in fact, a joke. I've tried using the google to find good jokes, but that's a needle-in-the-haystack fool's errand.

Admittedly, humor is tricky. Arguably, it is also a talent at least to some degree, which means people who feel they lack the talent might find this whole business intimidating. Fair enough. If you're not naturally funny, no one wants you to try to be funny. Trust me on that. Few things are as collectively uncomfortable as the communal silence following a joke that lands with a thud. It's perhaps the oratorical equivalent of leaving your fly open, causing everyone to feel red-faced on your behalf. I know this because I've done both and they feel remarkably alike. The assembly will quickly move from appreciating you to pitying you.

Pathetic pity is not the energy you want to drive into your message.

However, there is a subtle but important difference between being funny and being humorous. In fact, I'll go ahead and postulate that there's actually no real benefit to being funny at all, but a huge benefit to bringing humor. You don't have to be a comedian to find ways to bring good humor to homilies, ways to draw out smiles and joy if not audible laughter. And that's more than enough. Often, it's preferable. The goal of humor is to uplift spirits, not necessarily to make people laugh out loud. Sometimes, the most effective humor simply causes people to smile and open their eyes a little wider. That's enough. There are a lot of ways to do that without inducing snorts and guffaws.

As a parallel, I have a remarkably miniscule talent for music, so I'd rather not be expected to stand before a community and sing. That would be cruel and uncomfortable for everyone. But there is a moon-sized difference between not singing and not sharing music. I have a deep appreciation for music and routinely include musical references in my preaching, building off the poetry of songwriters. One of the most well-received and remembered homilies I ever gave unpacked the apocalyptic allegory of Don McClain's "American Pie." The music came alive in everyone's heart and head even though the preacher, thankfully, made no attempt to sing any of it.

A Few Things Worth Hanging On To

- "If humor without faith is in danger of dissolving into cynicism and despair, faith without humor is in danger of turning into arrogance and intolerance." (Conrad Hyers)

- Humor, especially self-deprecating humor, keeps the homilist humble and human. People relate to humble human homilists.

- Laughter is a social expression. It bonds people together and builds community.

- Humor relaxes people and opens them up. It helps them lower their ego defenses so their hearts and spirits can be engaged and perhaps even moved.

- You don't have to be funny or tell jokes to invoke humor. Enticing smiles and uplifting joy gets the job done just as well, perhaps even better.

Bringing It Home

MY DAD MOVED THE RIP FENCE TO THE LEFT SIDE OF THE BLADE AND SET UP TO FEED HIS PIECE FROM THE BACK-SIDE OF THE SAW. I tilted my head, furrowed my brow, and winced. This didn't look like a good idea. But who was I to question? My father was a very accomplished and skilled finish carpenter. His work was showcased in some of the most expensive and lavish homes throughout the city. He knew what he was doing. Everything I knew about wood-working and craftsmanship, I learned from him. And his relentless focus on safety had been drilled into me since I was old enough to swing a plastic hammer. The man tolerated zero safety compromises in the workshop or on a job site, and he took great pride that no one on any of his crews ever suffered a serious injury. Once, I saw him cut the cord of a circular saw while a guy was using it because he noticed the cord's insulated covering was compromised and fraying. He put the saw unquestionably out of commission until the cord was repaired.

What I watched him do with that table saw gave me pause. It didn't look safe, but who was I to question the master?

113

Contrarily, perhaps if I watched and paid attention I could learn a new technique for making a difficult cut.

He moved slowly, meticulously. It was a small piece and the backside of the blade's rotation would be pulling the wood away from the table's surface, so he used a push stick in his left hand to hold his work in place while he fed it into the saw with his right hand. He was an artist in action. Slowly, carefully, thoughtfully. Then, in the fraction of an instant, a chunk of wood shot across the shop like a missile and he, with arm flailing, jumped back from the saw, holding a bleeding thumb.

I leapt forward and killed the saw. "Are you OK?"

He stood with shock on his face, staring at a thumb hidden from my view by his other hand.

"Are you OK?" I asked a second time.

This time he answered, "Yes." His face was white, and I could tell his heart was racing. He took a breath. "I...OK... it's...just nicked the skin. It's OK."

I moved in to see for myself. Sure enough. He had gotten lucky. The saw's carbide teeth had only managed to chew through the top layer of skin. It needed no more treatment than a good washing and a Band-Aid. Color returned to his face.

"You're good?" I asked seeking reassurance.

"Yes, no problem."

"Good. Now it's my turn," I said, setting up the reversal of father/son roles. "That was the damn stupidest thing you've ever done. What in the hell were you even thinking? That was a bad idea from the get-go and you know better!"

"Well, I just thought..."

"Seems to me if you had thought at all you wouldn't have

tried that," I said, echoing the words I had heard him speak to me seven times seventy times before. As I spoke, I wondered about my motivation. He knew this, of course. He was the one standing there holding a bleeding thumb. The evidence was obvious. So why did I feel this need to express through my use of language what was already demonstrative before his eyes? He didn't need my correction; he needed my concern. I was merely indulging the smallest version of myself.

I learned two valuable lessons that day, all of which apply to life in general and extend to preaching homilies that bring meaningful and compelling value to people.

First, never take your skill for granted. Even the most experienced, gifted homilists are fully capable of bloodying their thumbs if they don't think things all the way through. We have to be really careful not to fall in love with our own ideas and become brainwashed by our own solutions, lest we fail to see the flaws. Nothing is automatically good simply because it comes from you. In fact, if you go back to our earlier chapters, you'll be reminded that nothing really good comes from us at all; it comes through us from the Holy Spirit.

For myself, personally, I find the process of preparing, writing, rewriting, re-rewriting, and re-re-rewriting to be very prayerful. If you pray at the beginning of your homily prep but not continuously throughout the development and writing process, you might want to rethink your approach. The Benedictines speak of prayer and work, recognizing that these two most important dimensions of life are, in fact, the same thing. I encourage you to avoid the temptation to compartmentalize your process. Writing is prayer and prayer is writing.

As a junior copywriter, I once asked an experienced, highly awarded senior writer what I needed to do to become as good as he was. Without missing a beat, he looked straight at me and said, "Never forget how bad you're capable of being, and then run like hell in the opposite direction." The opposite direction of my own worst is, of course, where God is found.

Second, comfort the afflicted and afflict the comfortable. I did these in reverse that day. In spite of his vigilance about safety, my dad had grown too comfortable around the table saw. I sensed it as he set up for the cut, but rather than challenge his thinking, I stood by and watched with interest. Did my intrigue inadvertently embolden his comfort? Should I have invited him to think again? I wouldn't have needed to challenge him; I could have simply engaged a dialog that would have compassionately afflicted his comfort: "I don't think I would be comfortable making that cut. What other options are available?"

Typically, those who are comfortable don't like being afflicted. Most of us would rather slam our fingers in car doors than have our attitudes and decisions challenged or critiqued. Self-righteousness and self-satisfaction feel so good! Yet, one of the roles of the homilist is to do just that. It takes finesse to invite the dialog without making an accusation or arousing defensiveness. It also helps to assign the issue to the self, admitting that you, the homilist, participate in the tension.

In criticizing my dad's decision after the fact, I learned how empty and unsatisfying it is to point out the errors of someone else's ways. Sure, it feels good in the moment, feeding the ego's desire to be righteous and settle past scores.

But what good does it ultimately do? People who are afflicted know they're afflicted. They do not need to be berated, shamed, or criticized for it. They know. Consider these two approaches of a father speaking to a son who failed Algebra II after not doing his homework.

1. I told you this would happen, but you wouldn't listen. This failure is the direct result of your laziness, so you had better get your act together right now! This is unacceptable and irresponsible. No college will even look at a kid who ignores his homework and then flunks out!

2. Well, this stings, doesn't it? I know because I've had plenty of my own failures along the way. We replay things in or heads and beat ourselves up over everything we wish we would have done differently. But the bigger question lies ahead: What can we take from this to ensure a better outcome in the future? Character is not defined by our failures; it's defined by how we respond. And you are a young man of strong character. I believe in you.

The first example above afflicted the afflicted; the second comforted the afflicted. Which father has a better relationship with his son? Which son is more likely to come to his father for advice in the future? Which is controlling and which is inspiring?

I think you got it from here.

To move a mountain,

nudge a heart

stir a soul.

The mountain

will notice

and follow on

its own.